THE WISDOM OF KING SOLOMON

A Volume Containing

Proverbs (KJV)

Ecclesiastes (KJV)

The Wisdom of Solomon (Vulgate)

The Song of Solomon (KJV)

The Psalms of Solomon (Harris), and

The Odes of Solomon (Harris)

Excerpted from the King James Version, St. Jerome's Vulgate
and J. Rendel Harris' Apocryphal Translations

Compiled and Edited by
Dennis Logan

Copyright 2020 by Rolled Scroll Publishing
ISBN: 9781952900204

Dedication

To my sons, daughters, nieces, nephews

And all the generations of today and tomorrow

May we aspire to Righteousness;

not for reward or merit,

but as a way of life.

Table of Contents

Proverbs 7

Ecclesiastes, or The Preacher 99

The Wisdom of Solomon 127

The Song of Solomon (The Song of Songs)........ 181

The Psalms of Solomon 196

The Odes of Solomon 233

Proverbs

(King James Version)

Chapter 1

1 The proverbs of Solomon the son of David, king of Israel;

2 To know wisdom and instruction; to perceive the words of understanding;

3 To receive the instruction of wisdom, justice, and judgment, and equity;

4 To give subtilty to the simple, to the young man knowledge and discretion.

5 A wise man will hear, and will increase learning; and a man of understanding shall attain unto wise counsels:

6 To understand a proverb, and the interpretation; the words of the wise, and their dark sayings.

7 The fear of the LORD is the beginning of knowledge: but fools despise wisdom and instruction.

8 My son, hear the instruction of thy father, and forsake not the law of thy mother:

9 For they shall be an ornament of grace unto thy head, and chains about thy neck.

10 My son, if sinners entice thee, consent thou not.

11 If they say, Come with us, let us lay wait for blood, let us lurk privily for the innocent without cause:

12 Let us swallow them up alive as the grave; and whole, as those that go down into the pit:

13 We shall find all precious substance, we shall fill our houses with spoil:

14 Cast in thy lot among us; let us all have one purse:

15 My son, walk not thou in the way with them; refrain thy foot from their path:

16 For their feet run to evil, and make haste to shed blood.

17 Surely in vain the net is spread in the sight of any bird.

18 And they lay wait for their own blood; they lurk privily for their own lives.

19 So are the ways of every one that is greedy of gain; which taketh away the life of the owners thereof.

20 Wisdom crieth without; she uttereth her voice in the streets:

21 She crieth in the chief place of concourse, in the openings of the gates: in the city she uttereth her words, saying,

22 How long, ye simple ones, will ye love simplicity? and the scorners delight in their scorning, and fools hate knowledge?

23 Turn you at my reproof: behold, I will pour out my spirit unto you, I will make known my words unto you.

24 Because I have called, and ye refused; I have stretched out my hand, and no man regarded;

25 But ye have set at nought all my counsel, and would none of my reproof:

26 I also will laugh at your calamity; I will mock when your fear cometh;

27 When your fear cometh as desolation, and your destruction cometh as a whirlwind; when distress and anguish cometh upon you.

28 Then shall they call upon me, but I will not answer; they shall seek me early, but they shall not find me:

29 For that they hated knowledge, and did not choose the fear of the LORD:

30 They would none of my counsel: they despised all my reproof.

31 Therefore shall they eat of the fruit of their own way, and be filled with their own devices.

32 For the turning away of the simple shall slay them, and the prosperity of fools shall destroy them.

33 But whoso hearkeneth unto me shall dwell safely, and shall be quiet from fear of evil.

Chapter 2

1 My son, if thou wilt receive my words, and hide my commandments with thee;

2 So that thou incline thine ear unto wisdom, and apply thine heart to understanding;

3 Yea, if thou criest after knowledge, and liftest up thy voice for understanding;

4 If thou seekest her as silver, and searchest for her as for hid treasures;

5 Then shalt thou understand the fear of the LORD, and find the knowledge of God.

6 For the LORD giveth wisdom: out of his mouth cometh knowledge and understanding.

7 He layeth up sound wisdom for the righteous: he is a buckler to them that walk uprightly.

8 He keepeth the paths of judgment, and preserveth the way of his saints.

9 Then shalt thou understand righteousness, and judgment, and equity; yea, every good path.

10 When wisdom entereth into thine heart, and knowledge is pleasant unto thy soul;

11 Discretion shall preserve thee, understanding shall keep thee:

12 To deliver thee from the way of the evil man, from the man that speaketh froward things;

13 Who leave the paths of uprightness, to walk in the ways of darkness;

14 Who rejoice to do evil, and delight in the frowardness of the wicked;

15 Whose ways are crooked, and they froward in their paths:

16 To deliver thee from the strange woman, even from the stranger which flattereth with her words;

17 Which forsaketh the guide of her youth, and forgetteth the covenant of her God.

18 For her house inclineth unto death, and her paths unto the dead.

19 None that go unto her return again, neither take they hold of the paths of life.

20 That thou mayest walk in the way of good men, and keep the paths of the righteous.

21 For the upright shall dwell in the land, and the perfect shall remain in it.

22 But the wicked shall be cut off from the earth, and the transgressors shall be rooted out of it.

Chapter 3

1 My son, forget not my law; but let thine heart keep my commandments:

2 For length of days, and long life, and peace, shall they add to thee.

3 Let not mercy and truth forsake thee: bind them about thy neck; write them upon the table of thine heart:

4 So shalt thou find favour and good understanding in the sight of God and man.

5 Trust in the LORD with all thine heart; and lean not unto thine own understanding.

6 In all thy ways acknowledge him, and he shall direct thy paths.

7 Be not wise in thine own eyes: fear the LORD, and depart from evil.

8 It shall be health to thy navel, and marrow to thy bones.

9 Honour the LORD with thy substance, and with the firstfruits of all thine increase:

10 So shall thy barns be filled with plenty, and thy presses shall burst out with new wine.

11 My son, despise not the chastening of the LORD; neither be weary of his correction:

12 For whom the LORD loveth he correcteth; even as a father the son in whom he delighteth.

13 Happy is the man that findeth wisdom, and the man that getteth understanding.

14 For the merchandise of it is better than the merchandise of silver, and the gain thereof than fine gold.

15 She is more precious than rubies: and all the things thou canst desire are not to be compared unto her.

16 Length of days is in her right hand; and in her left hand riches and honour.

17 Her ways are ways of pleasantness, and all her paths are peace.

18 She is a tree of life to them that lay hold upon her: and happy is every one that retaineth her.

19 The LORD by wisdom hath founded the earth; by understanding hath he established the heavens.

20 By his knowledge the depths are broken up, and the clouds drop down the dew.

21 My son, let not them depart from thine eyes: keep sound wisdom and discretion:

22 So shall they be life unto thy soul, and grace to thy neck.

23 Then shalt thou walk in thy way safely, and thy foot shall not stumble.

24 When thou liest down, thou shalt not be afraid: yea, thou shalt lie down, and thy sleep shall be sweet.

25 Be not afraid of sudden fear, neither of the desolation of the wicked, when it cometh.

26 For the LORD shall be thy confidence, and shall keep thy foot from being taken.

27 Withhold not good from them to whom it is due, when it is in the power of thine hand to do it.

28 Say not unto thy neighbour, Go, and come again, and to morrow I will give; when thou hast it by thee.

29 Devise not evil against thy neighbour, seeing he dwelleth securely by thee.

30 Strive not with a man without cause, if he have done thee no harm.

31 Envy thou not the oppressor, and choose none of his ways.

32 For the froward is abomination to the LORD: but his secret is with the righteous.

33 The curse of the LORD is in the house of the wicked: but he blesseth the habitation of the just.

34 Surely he scorneth the scorners: but he giveth grace unto the lowly.

35 The wise shall inherit glory: but shame shall be the promotion of fools.

Chapter 4

1 Hear, ye children, the instruction of a father, and attend to know understanding.

2 For I give you good doctrine, forsake ye not my law.

3 For I was my father's son, tender and only beloved in the sight of my mother.

4 He taught me also, and said unto me, Let thine heart retain my words: keep my commandments, and live.

5 Get wisdom, get understanding: forget it not; neither decline from the words of my mouth.

6 Forsake her not, and she shall preserve thee: love her, and she shall keep thee.

7 Wisdom is the principal thing; therefore get wisdom: and with all thy getting get understanding.

8 Exalt her, and she shall promote thee: she shall bring thee to honour, when thou dost embrace her.

9 She shall give to thine head an ornament of grace: a crown of glory shall she deliver to thee.

10 Hear, O my son, and receive my sayings; and the years of thy life shall be many.

11 I have taught thee in the way of wisdom; I have led thee in right paths.

12 When thou goest, thy steps shall not be straitened; and when thou runnest, thou shalt not stumble.

13 Take fast hold of instruction; let her not go: keep her; for she is thy life.

14 Enter not into the path of the wicked, and go not in the way of evil men.

15 Avoid it, pass not by it, turn from it, and pass away.

16 For they sleep not, except they have done mischief; and their sleep is taken away, unless they cause some to fall.

17 For they eat the bread of wickedness, and drink the wine of violence.

18 But the path of the just is as the shining light, that shineth more and more unto the perfect day.

19 The way of the wicked is as darkness: they know not at what they stumble.

20 My son, attend to my words; incline thine ear unto my sayings.

21 Let them not depart from thine eyes; keep them in the midst of thine heart.

22 For they are life unto those that find them, and health to all their flesh.

23 Keep thy heart with all diligence; for out of it are the issues of life.

24 Put away from thee a froward mouth, and perverse lips put far from thee.

25 Let thine eyes look right on, and let thine eyelids look straight before thee.

26 Ponder the path of thy feet, and let all thy ways be established.

27 Turn not to the right hand nor to the left: remove thy foot from evil.

Chapter 5

1 My son, attend unto my wisdom, and bow thine ear to my understanding:

2 That thou mayest regard discretion, and that thy lips may keep knowledge.

3 For the lips of a strange woman drop as an honeycomb, and her mouth is smoother than oil:

4 But her end is bitter as wormwood, sharp as a two-edged sword.

5 Her feet go down to death; her steps take hold on hell.

6 Lest thou shouldest ponder the path of life, her ways are moveable, that thou canst not know them.

7 Hear me now therefore, O ye children, and depart not from the words of my mouth.

8 Remove thy way far from her, and come not nigh the door of her house:

9 Lest thou give thine honour unto others, and thy years unto the cruel:

10 Lest strangers be filled with thy wealth; and thy labours be in the house of a stranger;

11 And thou mourn at the last, when thy flesh and thy body are consumed,

12 And say, How have I hated instruction, and my heart despised reproof;

13 And have not obeyed the voice of my teachers, nor inclined mine ear to them that instructed me!

14 I was almost in all evil in the midst of the congregation and assembly.

15 Drink waters out of thine own cistern, and running waters out of thine own well.

16 Let thy fountains be dispersed abroad, and rivers of waters in the streets.

17 Let them be only thine own, and not strangers' with thee.

18 Let thy fountain be blessed: and rejoice with the wife of thy youth.

19 Let her be as the loving hind and pleasant roe; let her breasts satisfy thee at all times; and be thou ravished always with her love.

20 And why wilt thou, my son, be ravished with a strange woman, and embrace the bosom of a stranger?

21 For the ways of man are before the eyes of the LORD, and he pondereth all his goings.

22 His own iniquities shall take the wicked himself, and he shall be holden with the cords of his sins.

23 He shall die without instruction; and in the greatness of his folly he shall go astray.

Chapter 6

1 My son, if thou be surety for thy friend, if thou hast stricken thy hand with a stranger,

2 Thou art snared with the words of thy mouth, thou art taken with the words of thy mouth.

3 Do this now, my son, and deliver thyself, when thou art come into the hand of thy friend; go, humble thyself, and make sure thy friend.

4 Give not sleep to thine eyes, nor slumber to thine eyelids.

5 Deliver thyself as a roe from the hand of the hunter, and as a bird from the hand of the fowler.

6 Go to the ant, thou sluggard; consider her ways, and be wise:

7 Which having no guide, overseer, or ruler,

8 Provideth her meat in the summer, and gathereth her food in the harvest.

9 How long wilt thou sleep, O sluggard? when wilt thou arise out of thy sleep?

10 Yet a little sleep, a little slumber, a little folding of the hands to sleep:

11 So shall thy poverty come as one that travelleth, and thy want as an armed man.

12 A naughty person, a wicked man, walketh with a froward mouth.

13 He winketh with his eyes, he speaketh with his feet, he teacheth with his fingers;

14 Frowardness is in his heart, he deviseth mischief continually; he soweth discord.

15 Therefore shall his calamity come suddenly; suddenly shall he be broken without remedy.

16 These six things doth the LORD hate: yea, seven are an abomination unto him:

17 A proud look, a lying tongue, and hands that shed innocent blood,

18 An heart that deviseth wicked imaginations, feet that be swift in running to mischief,

19 A false witness that speaketh lies, and he that soweth discord among brethren.

20 My son, keep thy father's commandment, and forsake not the law of thy mother:

21 Bind them continually upon thine heart, and tie them about thy neck.

22 When thou goest, it shall lead thee; when thou sleepest, it shall keep thee; and when thou awakest, it shall talk with thee.

23 For the commandment is a lamp; and the law is light; and reproofs of instruction are the way of life:

24 To keep thee from the evil woman, from the flattery of the tongue of a strange woman.

25 Lust not after her beauty in thine heart; neither let her take thee with her eyelids.

26 For by means of a whorish woman a man is brought to a piece of bread: and the adultress will hunt for the precious life.

27 Can a man take fire in his bosom, and his clothes not be burned?

28 Can one go upon hot coals, and his feet not be burned?

29 So he that goeth in to his neighbour's wife; whosoever toucheth her shall not be innocent.

30 Men do not despise a thief, if he steal to satisfy his soul when he is hungry;

31 But if he be found, he shall restore sevenfold; he shall give all the substance of his house.

32 But whoso committeth adultery with a woman lacketh understanding: he that doeth it destroyeth his own soul.

33 A wound and dishonour shall he get; and his reproach shall not be wiped away.

34 For jealousy is the rage of a man: therefore he will not spare in the day of vengeance.

35 He will not regard any ransom; neither will he rest content, though thou givest many gifts.

Chapter 7

1 My son, keep my words, and lay up my commandments with thee.

2 Keep my commandments, and live; and my law as the apple of thine eye.

3 Bind them upon thy fingers, write them upon the table of thine heart.

4 Say unto wisdom, Thou art my sister; and call understanding thy kinswoman:

5 That they may keep thee from the strange woman, from the stranger which flattereth with her words.

6 For at the window of my house I looked through my casement,

7 And beheld among the simple ones, I discerned among the youths, a young man void of understanding,

8 Passing through the street near her corner; and he went the way to her house,

9 In the twilight, in the evening, in the black and dark night:

10 And, behold, there met him a woman with the attire of an harlot, and subtil of heart.

11 (She is loud and stubborn; her feet abide not in her house:

12 Now is she without, now in the streets, and lieth in wait at every corner.)

13 So she caught him, and kissed him, and with an impudent face said unto him,

14 I have peace offerings with me; this day have I payed my vows.

15 Therefore came I forth to meet thee, diligently to seek thy face, and I have found thee.

16 I have decked my bed with coverings of tapestry, with carved works, with fine linen of Egypt.

17 I have perfumed my bed with myrrh, aloes, and cinnamon.

18 Come, let us take our fill of love until the morning: let us solace ourselves with loves.

19 For the goodman is not at home, he is gone a long journey: 20 He hath taken a bag of money with him, and will come home at the day appointed.

21 With her much fair speech she caused him to yield, with the flattering of her lips she forced him.

22 He goeth after her straightway, as an ox goeth to the slaughter, or as a fool to the correction of the stocks;

23 Till a dart strike through his liver; as a bird hasteth to the snare, and knoweth not that it is for his life.

24 Hearken unto me now therefore, O ye children, and attend to the words of my mouth.

25 Let not thine heart decline to her ways, go not astray in her paths.

26 For she hath cast down many wounded: yea, many strong men have been slain by her.

27 Her house is the way to hell, going down to the chambers of death.

Chapter 8

1 Doth not wisdom cry? and understanding put forth her voice?

2 She standeth in the top of high places, by the way in the places of the paths.

3 She crieth at the gates, at the entry of the city, at the coming in at the doors.

4 Unto you, O men, I call; and my voice is to the sons of man.

5 O ye simple, understand wisdom: and, ye fools, be ye of an understanding heart.

6 Hear; for I will speak of excellent things; and the opening of my lips shall be right things.

7 For my mouth shall speak truth; and wickedness is an abomination to my lips.

8 All the words of my mouth are in righteousness; there is nothing froward or perverse in them.

9 They are all plain to him that understandeth, and right to them that find knowledge.

10 Receive my instruction, and not silver; and knowledge rather than choice gold.

11 For wisdom is better than rubies; and all the things that may be desired are not to be compared to it.

12 I wisdom dwell with prudence, and find out knowledge of witty inventions.

13 The fear of the LORD is to hate evil: pride, and arrogancy, and the evil way, and the froward mouth, do I hate.

14 Counsel is mine, and sound wisdom: I am understanding; I have strength.

15 By me kings reign, and princes decree justice.

16 By me princes rule, and nobles, even all the judges of the earth.

17 I love them that love me; and those that seek me early shall find me.

18 Riches and honour are with me; yea, durable riches and righteousness.

19 My fruit is better than gold, yea, than fine gold; and my revenue than choice silver.

20 I lead in the way of righteousness, in the midst of the paths of judgment:

21 That I may cause those that love me to inherit substance; and I will fill their treasures.

22 The LORD possessed me in the beginning of his way, before his works of old.

23 I was set up from everlasting, from the beginning, or ever the earth was.

24 When there were no depths, I was brought forth; when there were no fountains abounding with water.

25 Before the mountains were settled, before the hills was I brought forth:

26 While as yet he had not made the earth, nor the fields, nor the highest part of the dust of the world.

27 When he prepared the heavens, I was there: when he set a compass upon the face of the depth:

28 When he established the clouds above: when he strengthened the fountains of the deep:

29 When he gave to the sea his decree, that the waters should not pass his commandment: when he appointed the foundations of the earth:

30 Then I was by him, as one brought up with him: and I was daily his delight, rejoicing always before him;

31 Rejoicing in the habitable part of his earth; and my delights were with the sons of men.

32 Now therefore hearken unto me, O ye children: for blessed are they that keep my ways.

33 Hear instruction, and be wise, and refuse it not.

34 Blessed is the man that heareth me, watching daily at my gates, waiting at the posts of my doors.

35 For whoso findeth me findeth life, and shall obtain favour of the LORD.

36 But he that sinneth against me wrongeth his own soul: all they that hate me love death.

Chapter 9

1 Wisdom hath builded her house, she hath hewn out her seven pillars:

2 She hath killed her beasts; she hath mingled her wine; she hath also furnished her table.

3 She hath sent forth her maidens: she crieth upon the highest places of the city,

4 Whoso is simple, let him turn in hither: as for him that wanteth understanding, she saith to him,

5 Come, eat of my bread, and drink of the wine which I have mingled.

6 Forsake the foolish, and live; and go in the way of understanding.

7 He that reproveth a scorner getteth to himself shame: and he that rebuketh a wicked man getteth himself a blot.

8 Reprove not a scorner, lest he hate thee: rebuke a wise man, and he will love thee.

9 Give instruction to a wise man, and he will be yet wiser: teach a just man, and he will increase in learning.

10 The fear of the LORD is the beginning of wisdom: and the knowledge of the holy is understanding.

11 For by me thy days shall be multiplied, and the years of thy life shall be increased.

12 If thou be wise, thou shalt be wise for thyself: but if thou scornest, thou alone shalt bear it.

13 A foolish woman is clamorous: she is simple, and knoweth nothing.

14 For she sitteth at the door of her house, on a seat in the high places of the city,

15 To call passengers who go right on their ways:

16 Whoso is simple, let him turn in hither: and as for him that wanteth understanding, she saith to him,

17 Stolen waters are sweet, and bread eaten in secret is pleasant.

18 But he knoweth not that the dead are there; and that her guests are in the depths of hell.

Chapter 10

1 The proverbs of Solomon. A wise son maketh a glad father: but a foolish son is the heaviness of his mother.

2 Treasures of wickedness profit nothing: but righteousness delivereth from death.

3 The LORD will not suffer the soul of the righteous to famish: but he casteth away the substance of the wicked.

4 He becometh poor that dealeth with a slack hand: but the hand of the diligent maketh rich.

5 He that gathereth in summer is a wise son: but he that sleepeth in harvest is a son that causeth shame.

6 Blessings are upon the head of the just: but violence covereth the mouth of the wicked.

7 The memory of the just is blessed: but the name of the wicked shall rot.

8 The wise in heart will receive commandments: but a prating fool shall fall.

9 He that walketh uprightly walketh surely: but he that perverteth his ways shall be known.

10 He that winketh with the eye causeth sorrow: but a prating fool shall fall.

11 The mouth of a righteous man is a well of life: but violence covereth the mouth of the wicked.

12 Hatred stirreth up strifes: but love covereth all sins.

13 In the lips of him that hath understanding wisdom is found: but a rod is for the back of him that is void of understanding.

14 Wise men lay up knowledge: but the mouth of the foolish is near destruction.

15 The rich man's wealth is his strong city: the destruction of the poor is their poverty.

16 The labour of the righteous tendeth to life: the fruit of the wicked to sin.

17 He is in the way of life that keepeth instruction: but he that refuseth reproof erreth.

18 He that hideth hatred with lying lips, and he that uttereth a slander, is a fool.

19 In the multitude of words there wanteth not sin: but he that refraineth his lips is wise.

20 The tongue of the just is as choice silver: the heart of the wicked is little worth.

21 The lips of the righteous feed many: but fools die for want of wisdom.

22 The blessing of the LORD, it maketh rich, and he addeth no sorrow with it.

23 It is as sport to a fool to do mischief: but a man of understanding hath wisdom.

24 The fear of the wicked, it shall come upon him: but the desire of the righteous shall be granted.

25 As the whirlwind passeth, so is the wicked no more: but the righteous is an everlasting foundation.

26 As vinegar to the teeth, and as smoke to the eyes, so is the sluggard to them that send him.

27 The fear of the LORD prolongeth days: but the years of the wicked shall be shortened.

28 The hope of the righteous shall be gladness: but the expectation of the wicked shall perish.

29 The way of the LORD is strength to the upright: but destruction shall be to the workers of iniquity.

30 The righteous shall never be removed: but the wicked shall not inhabit the earth.

31 The mouth of the just bringeth forth wisdom: but the froward tongue shall be cut out.

32 The lips of the righteous know what is acceptable: but the mouth of the wicked speaketh frowardness.

Chapter 11

1 A false balance is abomination to the LORD: but a just weight is his delight.

2 When pride cometh, then cometh shame: but with the lowly is wisdom.

3 The integrity of the upright shall guide them: but the perverseness of transgressors shall destroy them.

4 Riches profit not in the day of wrath: but righteousness delivereth from death.

5 The righteousness of the perfect shall direct his way: but the wicked shall fall by his own wickedness.

6 The righteousness of the upright shall deliver them: but transgressors shall be taken in their own naughtiness.

7 When a wicked man dieth, his expectation shall perish: and the hope of unjust men perisheth.

8 The righteous is delivered out of trouble, and the wicked cometh in his stead.

9 An hypocrite with his mouth destroyeth his neighbour: but through knowledge shall the just be delivered.

10 When it goeth well with the righteous, the city rejoiceth: and when the wicked perish, there is shouting.

11 By the blessing of the upright the city is exalted: but it is overthrown by the mouth of the wicked.

12 He that is void of wisdom despiseth his neighbour: but a man of understanding holdeth his peace.

13 A talebearer revealeth secrets: but he that is of a faithful spirit concealeth the matter.

14 Where no counsel is, the people fall: but in the multitude of counsellors there is safety.

15 He that is surety for a stranger shall smart for it: and he that hateth suretiship is sure.

16 A gracious woman retaineth honour: and strong men retain riches.

17 The merciful man doeth good to his own soul: but he that is cruel troubleth his own flesh.

18 The wicked worketh a deceitful work: but to him that soweth righteousness shall be a sure reward.

19 As righteousness tendeth to life: so he that pursueth evil pursueth it to his own death.

20 They that are of a froward heart are abomination to the LORD: but such as are upright in their way are his delight.

21 Though hand join in hand, the wicked shall not be unpunished: but the seed of the righteous shall be delivered.

22 As a jewel of gold in a swine's snout, so is a fair woman which is without discretion.

23 The desire of the righteous is only good: but the expectation of the wicked is wrath.

24 There is that scattereth, and yet increaseth; and there is that withholdeth more than is meet, but it tendeth to poverty.

25 The liberal soul shall be made fat: and he that watereth shall be watered also himself.

26 He that withholdeth corn, the people shall curse him: but blessing shall be upon the head of him that selleth it.

27 He that diligently seeketh good procureth favour: but he that seeketh mischief, it shall come unto him.

28 He that trusteth in his riches shall fall; but the righteous shall flourish as a branch.

29 He that troubleth his own house shall inherit the wind: and the fool shall be servant to the wise of heart.

30 The fruit of the righteous is a tree of life; and he that winneth souls is wise.

31 Behold, the righteous shall be recompensed in the earth: much more the wicked and the sinner.

Chapter 12

1 Whoso loveth instruction loveth knowledge: but he that hateth reproof is brutish.

2 A good man obtaineth favour of the LORD: but a man of wicked devices will he condemn.

3 A man shall not be established by wickedness: but the root of the righteous shall not be moved.

4 A virtuous woman is a crown to her husband: but she that maketh ashamed is as rottenness in his bones.

5 The thoughts of the righteous are right: but the counsels of the wicked are deceit.

6 The words of the wicked are to lie in wait for blood: but the mouth of the upright shall deliver them.

7 The wicked are overthrown, and are not: but the house of the righteous shall stand.

8 A man shall be commended according to his wisdom: but he that is of a perverse heart shall be despised.

9 He that is despised, and hath a servant, is better than he that honoureth himself, and lacketh bread.

10 A righteous man regardeth the life of his beast: but the tender mercies of the wicked are cruel.

11 He that tilleth his land shall be satisfied with bread: but he that followeth vain persons is void of understanding.

12 The wicked desireth the net of evil men: but the root of the righteous yieldeth fruit.

13 The wicked is snared by the transgression of his lips: but the just shall come out of trouble.

14 A man shall be satisfied with good by the fruit of his mouth: and the recompence of a man's hands shall be rendered unto him.

15 The way of a fool is right in his own eyes: but he that hearkeneth unto counsel is wise.

16 A fool's wrath is presently known: but a prudent man covereth shame.

17 He that speaketh truth sheweth forth righteousness: but a false witness deceit.

18 There is that speaketh like the piercings of a sword: but the tongue of the wise is health.

19 The lip of truth shall be established for ever: but a lying tongue is but for a moment.

20 Deceit is in the heart of them that imagine evil: but to the counsellors of peace is joy.

21 There shall no evil happen to the just: but the wicked shall be filled with mischief.

22 Lying lips are abomination to the LORD: but they that deal truly are his delight.

23 A prudent man concealeth knowledge: but the heart of fools proclaimeth foolishness.

24 The hand of the diligent shall bear rule: but the slothful shall be under tribute.

25 Heaviness in the heart of man maketh it stoop: but a good word maketh it glad.

26 The righteous is more excellent than his neighbour: but the way of the wicked seduceth them.

27 The slothful man roasteth not that which he took in hunting: but the substance of a diligent man is precious.

28 In the way of righteousness is life: and in the pathway thereof there is no death.

Chapter 13

1 A wise son heareth his father's instruction: but a scorner heareth not rebuke.

2 A man shall eat good by the fruit of his mouth: but the soul of the transgressors shall eat violence.

3 He that keepeth his mouth keepeth his life: but he that openeth wide his lips shall have destruction.

4 The soul of the sluggard desireth, and hath nothing: but the soul of the diligent shall be made fat.

5 A righteous man hateth lying: but a wicked man is loathsome, and cometh to shame.

6 Righteousness keepeth him that is upright in the way: but wickedness overthroweth the sinner.

7 There is that maketh himself rich, yet hath nothing: there is that maketh himself poor, yet hath great riches.

8 The ransom of a man's life are his riches: but the poor heareth not rebuke.

9 The light of the righteous rejoiceth: but the lamp of the wicked shall be put out.

10 Only by pride cometh contention: but with the well advised is wisdom.

11 Wealth gotten by vanity shall be diminished: but he that gathereth by labour shall increase.

12 Hope deferred maketh the heart sick: but when the desire cometh, it is a tree of life.

13 Whoso despiseth the word shall be destroyed: but he that feareth the commandment shall be rewarded.

14 The law of the wise is a fountain of life, to depart from the snares of death.

15 Good understanding giveth favour: but the way of transgressors is hard.

16 Every prudent man dealeth with knowledge: but a fool layeth open his folly.

17 A wicked messenger falleth into mischief: but a faithful ambassador is health.

18 Poverty and shame shall be to him that refuseth instruction: but he that regardeth reproof shall be honoured.

19 The desire accomplished is sweet to the soul: but it is abomination to fools to depart from evil.

20 He that walketh with wise men shall be wise: but a companion of fools shall be destroyed.

21 Evil pursueth sinners: but to the righteous good shall be repayed.

22 A good man leaveth an inheritance to his children's children: and the wealth of the sinner is laid up for the just.

23 Much food is in the tillage of the poor: but there is that is destroyed for want of judgment.

24 He that spareth his rod hateth his son: but he that loveth him chasteneth him betimes.

25 The righteous eateth to the satisfying of his soul: but the belly of the wicked shall want.

Chapter 14

1 Every wise woman buildeth her house: but the foolish plucketh it down with her hands.

2 He that walketh in his uprightness feareth the LORD: but he that is perverse in his ways despiseth him.

3 In the mouth of the foolish is a rod of pride: but the lips of the wise shall preserve them.

4 Where no oxen are, the crib is clean: but much increase is by the strength of the ox.

5 A faithful witness will not lie: but a false witness will utter lies.

6 A scorner seeketh wisdom, and findeth it not: but knowledge is easy unto him that understandeth.

7 Go from the presence of a foolish man, when thou perceivest not in him the lips of knowledge.

8 The wisdom of the prudent is to understand his way: but the folly of fools is deceit.

9 Fools make a mock at sin: but among the righteous there is favour.

10 The heart knoweth his own bitterness; and a stranger doth not intermeddle with his joy.

11 The house of the wicked shall be overthrown: but the tabernacle of the upright shall flourish.

12 There is a way which seemeth right unto a man, but the end thereof are the ways of death.

13 Even in laughter the heart is sorrowful; and the end of that mirth is heaviness.

14 The backslider in heart shall be filled with his own ways: and a good man shall be satisfied from himself.

15 The simple believeth every word: but the prudent man looketh well to his going.

16 A wise man feareth, and departeth from evil: but the fool rageth, and is confident.

17 He that is soon angry dealeth foolishly: and a man of wicked devices is hated.

18 The simple inherit folly: but the prudent are crowned with knowledge.

19 The evil bow before the good; and the wicked at the gates of the righteous.

20 The poor is hated even of his own neighbour: but the rich hath many friends.

21 He that despiseth his neighbour sinneth: but he that hath mercy on the poor, happy is he.

22 Do they not err that devise evil? but mercy and truth shall be to them that devise good.

23 In all labour there is profit: but the talk of the lips tendeth only to penury.

24 The crown of the wise is their riches: but the foolishness of fools is folly.

25 A true witness delivereth souls: but a deceitful witness speaketh lies.

26 In the fear of the LORD is strong confidence: and his children shall have a place of refuge.

27 The fear of the LORD is a fountain of life, to depart from the snares of death.

28 In the multitude of people is the king's honour: but in the want of people is the destruction of the prince.

29 He that is slow to wrath is of great understanding: but he that is hasty of spirit exalteth folly.

30 A sound heart is the life of the flesh: but envy the rottenness of the bones.

31 He that oppresseth the poor reproacheth his Maker: but he that honoureth him hath mercy on the poor.

32 The wicked is driven away in his wickedness: but the righteous hath hope in his death.

33 Wisdom resteth in the heart of him that hath understanding: but that which is in the midst of fools is made known.

34 Righteousness exalteth a nation: but sin is a reproach to any people.

35 The king's favour is toward a wise servant: but his wrath is against him that causeth shame.

Chapter 15

1 A soft answer turneth away wrath: but grievous words stir up anger.

2 The tongue of the wise useth knowledge aright: but the mouth of fools poureth out foolishness.

3 The eyes of the LORD are in every place, beholding the evil and the good.

4 A wholesome tongue is a tree of life: but perverseness therein is a breach in the spirit.

5 A fool despiseth his father's instruction: but he that regardeth reproof is prudent.

6 In the house of the righteous is much treasure: but in the revenues of the wicked is trouble.

7 The lips of the wise disperse knowledge: but the heart of the foolish doeth not so.

8 The sacrifice of the wicked is an abomination to the LORD: but the prayer of the upright is his delight.

9 The way of the wicked is an abomination unto the LORD: but he loveth him that followeth after righteousness.

10 Correction is grievous unto him that forsaketh the way: and he that hateth reproof shall die.

11 Hell and destruction are before the LORD: how much more then the hearts of the children of men?

12 A scorner loveth not one that reproveth him: neither will he go unto the wise.

13 A merry heart maketh a cheerful countenance: but by sorrow of the heart the spirit is broken.

14 The heart of him that hath understanding seeketh knowledge: but the mouth of fools feedeth on foolishness.

15 All the days of the afflicted are evil: but he that is of a merry heart hath a continual feast.

16 Better is little with the fear of the LORD than great treasure and trouble therewith.

17 Better is a dinner of herbs where love is, than a stalled ox and hatred therewith.

18 A wrathful man stirreth up strife: but he that is slow to anger appeaseth strife.

19 The way of the slothful man is as an hedge of thorns: but the way of the righteous is made plain.

20 A wise son maketh a glad father: but a foolish man despiseth his mother.

21 Folly is joy to him that is destitute of wisdom: but a man of understanding walketh uprightly.

22 Without counsel purposes are disappointed: but in the multitude of counsellors they are established.

23 A man hath joy by the answer of his mouth: and a word spoken in due season, how good is it!

24 The way of life is above to the wise, that he may depart from hell beneath.

25 The LORD will destroy the house of the proud: but he will establish the border of the widow.

26 The thoughts of the wicked are an abomination to the LORD: but the words of the pure are pleasant words.

27 He that is greedy of gain troubleth his own house; but he that hateth gifts shall live.

28 The heart of the righteous studieth to answer: but the mouth of the wicked poureth out evil things.

29 The LORD is far from the wicked: but he heareth the prayer of the righteous.

30 The light of the eyes rejoiceth the heart: and a good report maketh the bones fat.

31 The ear that heareth the reproof of life abideth among the wise.

32 He that refuseth instruction despiseth his own soul: but he that heareth reproof getteth understanding.

33 The fear of the LORD is the instruction of wisdom; and before honour is humility.

Chapter 16

1 The preparations of the heart in man, and the answer of the tongue, is from the LORD.

2 All the ways of a man are clean in his own eyes; but the LORD weigheth the spirits.

3 Commit thy works unto the LORD, and thy thoughts shall be established.

4 The LORD hath made all things for himself: yea, even the wicked for the day of evil.

5 Every one that is proud in heart is an abomination to the LORD: though hand join in hand, he shall not be unpunished.

6 By mercy and truth iniquity is purged: and by the fear of the LORD men depart from evil.

7 When a man's ways please the LORD, he maketh even his enemies to be at peace with him.

8 Better is a little with righteousness than great revenues without right.

9 A man's heart deviseth his way: but the LORD directeth his steps.

10 A divine sentence is in the lips of the king: his mouth transgresseth not in judgment.

11 A just weight and balance are the LORD's: all the weights of the bag are his work.

12 It is an abomination to kings to commit wickedness: for the throne is established by righteousness.

13 Righteous lips are the delight of kings; and they love him that speaketh right.

14 The wrath of a king is as messengers of death: but a wise man will pacify it.

15 In the light of the king's countenance is life; and his favour is as a cloud of the latter rain.

16 How much better is it to get wisdom than gold! and to get understanding rather to be chosen than silver!

17 The highway of the upright is to depart from evil: he that keepeth his way preserveth his soul.

18 Pride goeth before destruction, and an haughty spirit before a fall.

19 Better it is to be of an humble spirit with the lowly, than to divide the spoil with the proud.

20 He that handleth a matter wisely shall find good: and whoso trusteth in the LORD, happy is he.

21 The wise in heart shall be called prudent: and the sweetness of the lips increaseth learning.

22 Understanding is a wellspring of life unto him that hath it: but the instruction of fools is folly.

23 The heart of the wise teacheth his mouth, and addeth learning to his lips.

24 Pleasant words are as an honeycomb, sweet to the soul, and health to the bones.

25 There is a way that seemeth right unto a man, but the end thereof are the ways of death.

26 He that laboureth laboureth for himself; for his mouth craveth it of him.

27 An ungodly man diggeth up evil: and in his lips there is as a burning fire.

28 A froward man soweth strife: and a whisperer separateth chief friends.

29 A violent man enticeth his neighbour, and leadeth him into the way that is not good.

30 He shutteth his eyes to devise froward things: moving his lips he bringeth evil to pass.

31 The hoary head is a crown of glory, if it be found in the way of righteousness.

32 He that is slow to anger is better than the mighty; and he that ruleth his spirit than he that taketh a city.

33 The lot is cast into the lap; but the whole disposing thereof is of the LORD.

Chapter 17

1 Better is a dry morsel, and quietness therewith, than an house full of sacrifices with strife.

2 A wise servant shall have rule over a son that causeth shame, and shall have part of the inheritance among the brethren.

3 The fining pot is for silver, and the furnace for gold: but the LORD trieth the hearts.

4 A wicked doer giveth heed to false lips; and a liar giveth ear to a naughty tongue.

5 Whoso mocketh the poor reproacheth his Maker: and he that is glad at calamities shall not be unpunished.

6 Children's children are the crown of old men; and the glory of children are their fathers.

7 Excellent speech becometh not a fool: much less do lying lips a prince.

8 A gift is as a precious stone in the eyes of him that hath it: whithersoever it turneth, it prospereth.

9 He that covereth a transgression seeketh love; but he that repeateth a matter separateth very friends.

10 A reproof entereth more into a wise man than an hundred stripes into a fool.

11 An evil man seeketh only rebellion: therefore a cruel messenger shall be sent against him.

12 Let a bear robbed of her whelps meet a man, rather than a fool in his folly.

13 Whoso rewardeth evil for good, evil shall not depart from his house.

14 The beginning of strife is as when one letteth out water: therefore leave off contention, before it be meddled with.

15 He that justifieth the wicked, and he that condemneth the just, even they both are abomination to the LORD.

16 Wherefore is there a price in the hand of a fool to get wisdom, seeing he hath no heart to it?

17 A friend loveth at all times, and a brother is born for adversity.

18 A man void of understanding striketh hands, and becometh surety in the presence of his friend.

19 He loveth transgression that loveth strife: and he that exalteth his gate seeketh destruction.

20 He that hath a froward heart findeth no good: and he that hath a perverse tongue falleth into mischief.

21 He that begetteth a fool doeth it to his sorrow: and the father of a fool hath no joy.

22 A merry heart doeth good like a medicine: but a broken spirit drieth the bones.

23 A wicked man taketh a gift out of the bosom to pervert the ways of judgment.

24 Wisdom is before him that hath understanding; but the eyes of a fool are in the ends of the earth.

25 A foolish son is a grief to his father, and bitterness to her that bare him.

26 Also to punish the just is not good, nor to strike princes for equity.

27 He that hath knowledge spareth his words: and a man of understanding is of an excellent spirit.

28 Even a fool, when he holdeth his peace, is counted wise: and he that shutteth his lips is esteemed a man of understanding.

Chapter 18

1 Through desire a man, having separated himself, seeketh and intermeddleth with all wisdom.

2 A fool hath no delight in understanding, but that his heart may discover itself.

3 When the wicked cometh, then cometh also contempt, and with ignominy reproach.

4 The words of a man's mouth are as deep waters, and the wellspring of wisdom as a flowing brook.

5 It is not good to accept the person of the wicked, to overthrow the righteous in judgment.

6 A fool's lips enter into contention, and his mouth calleth for strokes.

7 A fool's mouth is his destruction, and his lips are the snare of his soul.

8 The words of a talebearer are as wounds, and they go down into the innermost parts of the belly.

9 He also that is slothful in his work is brother to him that is a great waster.

10 The name of the LORD is a strong tower: the righteous runneth into it, and is safe.

11 The rich man's wealth is his strong city, and as an high wall in his own conceit.

12 Before destruction the heart of man is haughty, and before honour is humility.

13 He that answereth a matter before he heareth it, it is folly and shame unto him.

14 The spirit of a man will sustain his infirmity; but a wounded spirit who can bear? 15 The heart of the prudent getteth knowledge; and the ear of the wise seeketh knowledge.

16 A man's gift maketh room for him, and bringeth him before great men.

17 He that is first in his own cause seemeth just; but his neighbour cometh and searcheth him.

18 The lot causeth contentions to cease, and parteth between the mighty.

19 A brother offended is harder to be won than a strong city: and their contentions are like the bars of a castle.

20 A man's belly shall be satisfied with the fruit of his mouth; and with the increase of his lips shall he be filled.

21 Death and life are in the power of the tongue: and they that love it shall eat the fruit thereof.

22 Whoso findeth a wife findeth a good thing, and obtaineth favour of the LORD.

23 The poor useth intreaties; but the rich answereth roughly.

24 A man that hath friends must shew himself friendly: and there is a friend that sticketh closer than a brother.

Chapter 19

1 Better is the poor that walketh in his integrity, than he that is perverse in his lips, and is a fool.

2 Also, that the soul be without knowledge, it is not good; and he that hasteth with his feet sinneth.

3 The foolishness of man perverteth his way: and his heart fretteth against the LORD.

4 Wealth maketh many friends; but the poor is separated from his neighbour.

5 A false witness shall not be unpunished, and he that speaketh lies shall not escape.

6 Many will intreat the favour of the prince: and every man is a friend to him that giveth gifts.

7 All the brethren of the poor do hate him: how much more do his friends go far from him? he pursueth them with words, yet they are wanting to him.

8 He that getteth wisdom loveth his own soul: he that keepeth understanding shall find good.

9 A false witness shall not be unpunished, and he that speaketh lies shall perish.

10 Delight is not seemly for a fool; much less for a servant to have rule over princes.

11 The discretion of a man deferreth his anger; and it is his glory to pass over a transgression.

12 The king's wrath is as the roaring of a lion; but his favour is as dew upon the grass.

13 A foolish son is the calamity of his father: and the contentions of a wife are a continual dropping.

14 House and riches are the inheritance of fathers: and a prudent wife is from the LORD.

15 Slothfulness casteth into a deep sleep; and an idle soul shall suffer hunger.

16 He that keepeth the commandment keepeth his own soul; but he that despiseth his ways shall die.

17 He that hath pity upon the poor lendeth unto the LORD; and that which he hath given will he pay him again.

18 Chasten thy son while there is hope, and let not thy soul spare for his crying.

19 A man of great wrath shall suffer punishment: for if thou deliver him, yet thou must do it again.

20 Hear counsel, and receive instruction, that thou mayest be wise in thy latter end.

21 There are many devices in a man's heart; nevertheless the counsel of the LORD, that shall stand.

22 The desire of a man is his kindness: and a poor man is better than a liar.

23 The fear of the LORD tendeth to life: and he that hath it shall abide satisfied; he shall not be visited with evil.

24 A slothful man hideth his hand in his bosom, and will not so much as bring it to his mouth again.

25 Smite a scorner, and the simple will beware: and reprove one that hath understanding, and he will understand knowledge.

26 He that wasteth his father, and chaseth away his mother, is a son that causeth shame, and bringeth reproach.

27 Cease, my son, to hear the instruction that causeth to err from the words of knowledge.

28 An ungodly witness scorneth judgment: and the mouth of the wicked devoureth iniquity.

29 Judgments are prepared for scorners, and stripes for the back of fools.

Chapter 20

1 Wine is a mocker, strong drink is raging: and whosoever is deceived thereby is not wise.

2 The fear of a king is as the roaring of a lion: whoso provoketh him to anger sinneth against his own soul.

3 It is an honour for a man to cease from strife: but every fool will be meddling.

4 The sluggard will not plow by reason of the cold; therefore shall he beg in harvest, and have nothing.

5 Counsel in the heart of man is like deep water; but a man of understanding will draw it out.

6 Most men will proclaim every one his own goodness: but a faithful man who can find? 7 The just man walketh in his integrity: his children are blessed after him.

8 A king that sitteth in the throne of judgment scattereth away all evil with his eyes.

9 Who can say, I have made my heart clean, I am pure from my sin? 10 Divers weights, and divers measures, both of them are alike abomination to the LORD.

11 Even a child is known by his doings, whether his work be pure, and whether it be right.

12 The hearing ear, and the seeing eye, the LORD hath made even both of them.

13 Love not sleep, lest thou come to poverty; open thine eyes, and thou shalt be satisfied with bread.

14 It is naught, it is naught, saith the buyer: but when he is gone his way, then he boasteth.

15 There is gold, and a multitude of rubies: but the lips of knowledge are a precious jewel.

16 Take his garment that is surety for a stranger: and take a pledge of him for a strange woman.

17 Bread of deceit is sweet to a man; but afterwards his mouth shall be filled with gravel.

18 Every purpose is established by counsel: and with good advice make war.

19 He that goeth about as a talebearer revealeth secrets: therefore meddle not with him that flattereth with his lips.

20 Whoso curseth his father or his mother, his lamp shall be put out in obscure darkness.

21 An inheritance may be gotten hastily at the beginning; but the end thereof shall not be blessed.

22 Say not thou, I will recompense evil; but wait on the LORD, and he shall save thee.

23 Divers weights are an abomination unto the LORD; and a false balance is not good.

24 Man's goings are of the LORD; how can a man then understand his own way?

25 It is a snare to the man who devoureth that which is holy, and after vows to make enquiry.

26 A wise king scattereth the wicked, and bringeth the wheel over them.

27 The spirit of man is the candle of the LORD, searching all the inward parts of the belly.

28 Mercy and truth preserve the king: and his throne is upholden by mercy.

29 The glory of young men is their strength: and the beauty of old men is the grey head.

30 The blueness of a wound cleanseth away evil: so do stripes the inward parts of the belly.

Chapter 21

1 The king's heart is in the hand of the LORD, as the rivers of water: he turneth it whithersoever he will.

2 Every way of a man is right in his own eyes: but the LORD pondereth the hearts.

3 To do justice and judgment is more acceptable to the LORD than sacrifice.

4 An high look, and a proud heart, and the plowing of the wicked, is sin.

5 The thoughts of the diligent tend only to plenteousness; but of every one that is hasty only to want.

6 The getting of treasures by a lying tongue is a vanity tossed to and fro of them that seek death.

7 The robbery of the wicked shall destroy them; because they refuse to do judgment.

8 The way of man is froward and strange: but as for the pure, his work is right.

9 It is better to dwell in a corner of the housetop, than with a brawling woman in a wide house.

10 The soul of the wicked desireth evil: his neighbour findeth no favour in his eyes.

11 When the scorner is punished, the simple is made wise: and when the wise is instructed, he receiveth knowledge.

12 The righteous man wisely considereth the house of the wicked: but God overthroweth the wicked for their wickedness.

13 Whoso stoppeth his ears at the cry of the poor, he also shall cry himself, but shall not be heard.

14 A gift in secret pacifieth anger: and a reward in the bosom strong wrath.

15 It is joy to the just to do judgment: but destruction shall be to the workers of iniquity.

16 The man that wandereth out of the way of understanding shall remain in the congregation of the dead.

17 He that loveth pleasure shall be a poor man: he that loveth wine and oil shall not be rich.

18 The wicked shall be a ransom for the righteous, and the transgressor for the upright.

19 It is better to dwell in the wilderness, than with a contentious and an angry woman.

20 There is treasure to be desired and oil in the dwelling of the wise; but a foolish man spendeth it up.

21 He that followeth after righteousness and mercy findeth life, righteousness, and honour.

22 A wise man scaleth the city of the mighty, and casteth down the strength of the confidence thereof.

23 Whoso keepeth his mouth and his tongue keepeth his soul from troubles.

24 Proud and haughty scorner is his name, who dealeth in proud wrath.

25 The desire of the slothful killeth him; for his hands refuse to labour.

26 He coveteth greedily all the day long: but the righteous giveth and spareth not.

27 The sacrifice of the wicked is abomination: how much more, when he bringeth it with a wicked mind?

28 A false witness shall perish: but the man that heareth speaketh constantly.

29 A wicked man hardeneth his face: but as for the upright, he directeth his way.

30 There is no wisdom nor understanding nor counsel against the LORD.

31 The horse is prepared against the day of battle: but safety is of the LORD.

Chapter 22

1 A GOOD name is rather to be chosen than great riches, and loving favour rather than silver and gold.

2 The rich and poor meet together: the LORD is the maker of them all.

3 A prudent man foreseeth the evil, and hideth himself: but the simple pass on, and are punished.

4 By humility and the fear of the LORD are riches, and honour, and life.

5 Thorns and snares are in the way of the froward: he that doth keep his soul shall be far from them.

6 Train up a child in the way he should go: and when he is old, he will not depart from it.

7 The rich ruleth over the poor, and the borrower is servant to the lender.

8 He that soweth iniquity shall reap vanity: and the rod of his anger shall fail.

9 He that hath a bountiful eye shall be blessed; for he giveth of his bread to the poor.

10 Cast out the scorner, and contention shall go out; yea, strife and reproach shall cease.

11 He that loveth pureness of heart, for the grace of his lips the king shall be his friend.

12 The eyes of the LORD preserve knowledge, and he overthroweth the words of the transgressor.

13 The slothful man saith, There is a lion without, I shall be slain in the streets.

14 The mouth of strange women is a deep pit: he that is abhorred of the LORD shall fall therein.

15 Foolishness is bound in the heart of a child; but the rod of correction shall drive it far from him.

16 He that oppresseth the poor to increase his riches, and he that giveth to the rich, shall surely come to want.

17 Bow down thine ear, and hear the words of the wise, and apply thine heart unto my knowledge.

18 For it is a pleasant thing if thou keep them within thee; they shall withal be fitted in thy lips.

19 That thy trust may be in the LORD, I have made known to thee this day, even to thee.

20 Have not I written to thee excellent things in counsels and knowledge,

21 That I might make thee know the certainty of the words of truth; that thou mightest answer the words of truth to them that send unto thee?

22 Rob not the poor, because he is poor: neither oppress the afflicted in the gate:

23 For the LORD will plead their cause, and spoil the soul of those that spoiled them.

24 Make no friendship with an angry man; and with a furious man thou shalt not go:

25 Lest thou learn his ways, and get a snare to thy soul.

26 Be not thou one of them that strike hands, or of them that are sureties for debts.

27 If thou hast nothing to pay, why should he take away thy bed from under thee? 28 Remove not the ancient landmark, which thy fathers have set.

29 Seest thou a man diligent in his business? he shall stand before kings; he shall not stand before mean men.

Chapter 23

1 When thou sittest to eat with a ruler, consider diligently what is before thee:

2 And put a knife to thy throat, if thou be a man given to appetite.

3 Be not desirous of his dainties: for they are deceitful meat.

4 Labour not to be rich: cease from thine own wisdom.

5 Wilt thou set thine eyes upon that which is not? for riches certainly make themselves wings; they fly away as an eagle toward heaven.

6 Eat thou not the bread of him that hath an evil eye, neither desire thou his dainty meats:

7 For as he thinketh in his heart, so is he: Eat and drink, saith he to thee; but his heart is not with thee.

8 The morsel which thou hast eaten shalt thou vomit up, and lose thy sweet words.

9 Speak not in the ears of a fool: for he will despise the wisdom of thy words.

10 Remove not the old landmark; and enter not into the fields of the fatherless:

11 For their redeemer is mighty; he shall plead their cause with thee.

12 Apply thine heart unto instruction, and thine ears to the words of knowledge.

13 Withhold not correction from the child: for if thou beatest him with the rod, he shall not die.

14 Thou shalt beat him with the rod, and shalt deliver his soul from hell.

15 My son, if thine heart be wise, my heart shall rejoice, even mine.

16 Yea, my reins shall rejoice, when thy lips speak right things.

17 Let not thine heart envy sinners: but be thou in the fear of the LORD all the day long.

18 For surely there is an end; and thine expectation shall not be cut off.

19 Hear thou, my son, and be wise, and guide thine heart in the way.

20 Be not among winebibbers; among riotous eaters of flesh:

21 For the drunkard and the glutton shall come to poverty: and drowsiness shall clothe a man with rags.

22 Hearken unto thy father that begat thee, and despise not thy mother when she is old.

23 Buy the truth, and sell it not; also wisdom, and instruction, and understanding.

24 The father of the righteous shall greatly rejoice: and he that begetteth a wise child shall have joy of him.

25 Thy father and thy mother shall be glad, and she that bare thee shall rejoice.

26 My son, give me thine heart, and let thine eyes observe my ways.

27 For a whore is a deep ditch; and a strange woman is a narrow pit.

28 She also lieth in wait as for a prey, and increaseth the transgressors among men.

29 Who hath woe? who hath sorrow? who hath contentions? who hath babbling? who hath wounds without cause? who hath redness of eyes?

30 They that tarry long at the wine; they that go to seek mixed wine.

31 Look not thou upon the wine when it is red, when it giveth his colour in the cup, when it moveth itself aright.

32 At the last it biteth like a serpent, and stingeth like an adder.

33 Thine eyes shall behold strange women, and thine heart shall utter perverse things.

34 Yea, thou shalt be as he that lieth down in the midst of the sea, or as he that lieth upon the top of a mast.

35 They have stricken me, shalt thou say, and I was not sick; they have beaten me, and I felt it not: when shall I awake? I will seek it yet again.

Chapter 24

1 Be not thou envious against evil men, neither desire to be with them.

2 For their heart studieth destruction, and their lips talk of mischief.

3 Through wisdom is an house builded; and by understanding it is established: 4 And by knowledge shall the chambers be filled with all precious and pleasant riches.

5 A wise man is strong; yea, a man of knowledge increaseth strength.

6 For by wise counsel thou shalt make thy war: and in multitude of counsellors there is safety.

7 Wisdom is too high for a fool: he openeth not his mouth in the gate.

8 He that deviseth to do evil shall be called a mischievous person.

9 The thought of foolishness is sin: and the scorner is an abomination to men.

10 If thou faint in the day of adversity, thy strength is small.

11 If thou forbear to deliver them that are drawn unto death, and those that are ready to be slain;

12 If thou sayest, Behold, we knew it not; doth not he that pondereth the heart consider it? and he that keepeth thy soul, doth not he know it? and shall not he render to every man according to his works?

13 My son, eat thou honey, because it is good; and the honeycomb, which is sweet to thy taste:

14 So shall the knowledge of wisdom be unto thy soul: when thou hast found it, then there shall be a reward, and thy expectation shall not be cut off.

15 Lay not wait, O wicked man, against the dwelling of the righteous; spoil not his resting place:

16 For a just man falleth seven times, and riseth up again: but the wicked shall fall into mischief.

17 Rejoice not when thine enemy falleth, and let not thine heart be glad when he stumbleth:

18 Lest the LORD see it, and it displease him, and he turn away his wrath from him.

19 Fret not thyself because of evil men, neither be thou envious at the wicked:

20 For there shall be no reward to the evil man; the candle of the wicked shall be put out.

21 My son, fear thou the LORD and the king: and meddle not with them that are given to change:

22 For their calamity shall rise suddenly; and who knoweth the ruin of them both?

23 These things also belong to the wise. It is not good to have respect of persons in judgment.

24 He that saith unto the wicked, Thou are righteous; him shall the people curse, nations shall abhor him:

25 But to them that rebuke him shall be delight, and a good blessing shall come upon them.

26 Every man shall kiss his lips that giveth a right answer.

27 Prepare thy work without, and make it fit for thyself in the field; and afterwards build thine house.

28 Be not a witness against thy neighbour without cause; and deceive not with thy lips.

29 Say not, I will do so to him as he hath done to me: I will render to the man according to his work.

30 I went by the field of the slothful, and by the vineyard of the man void of understanding;

31 And, lo, it was all grown over with thorns, and nettles had covered the face thereof, and the stone wall thereof was broken down.

32 Then I saw, and considered it well: I looked upon it, and received instruction.

33 Yet a little sleep, a little slumber, a little folding of the hands to sleep:

34 So shall thy poverty come as one that travelleth; and thy want as an armed man.

Chapter 25

1 These are also proverbs of Solomon, which the men of Hezekiah king of Judah copied out.

2 It is the glory of God to conceal a thing: but the honour of kings is to search out a matter.

3 The heaven for height, and the earth for depth, and the heart of kings is unsearchable.

4 Take away the dross from the silver, and there shall come forth a vessel for the finer.

5 Take away the wicked from before the king, and his throne shall be established in righteousness.

6 Put not forth thyself in the presence of the king, and stand not in the place of great men:

7 For better it is that it be said unto thee, Come up hither; than that thou shouldest be put lower in the presence of the prince whom thine eyes have seen.

8 Go not forth hastily to strive, lest thou know not what to do in the end thereof, when thy neighbour hath put thee to shame.

9 Debate thy cause with thy neighbour himself; and discover not a secret to another:

10 Lest he that heareth it put thee to shame, and thine infamy turn not away.

11 A word fitly spoken is like apples of gold in pictures of silver.

12 As an earring of gold, and an ornament of fine gold, so is a wise reprover upon an obedient ear.

13 As the cold of snow in the time of harvest, so is a faithful messenger to them that send him: for he refresheth the soul of his masters.

14 Whoso boasteth himself of a false gift is like clouds and wind without rain.

15 By long forbearing is a prince persuaded, and a soft tongue breaketh the bone.

16 Hast thou found honey? eat so much as is sufficient for thee, lest thou be filled therewith, and vomit it.

17 Withdraw thy foot from thy neighbour's house; lest he be weary of thee, and so hate thee.

18 A man that beareth false witness against his neighbour is a maul, and a sword, and a sharp arrow.

19 Confidence in an unfaithful man in time of trouble is like a broken tooth, and a foot out of joint.

20 As he that taketh away a garment in cold weather, and as vinegar upon nitre, so is he that singeth songs to an heavy heart.

21 If thine enemy be hungry, give him bread to eat; and if he be thirsty, give him water to drink:

22 For thou shalt heap coals of fire upon his head, and the LORD shall reward thee.

23 The north wind driveth away rain: so doth an angry countenance a backbiting tongue.

24 It is better to dwell in the corner of the housetop, than with a brawling woman and in a wide house.

25 As cold waters to a thirsty soul, so is good news from a far country.

26 A righteous man falling down before the wicked is as a troubled fountain, and a corrupt spring.

27 It is not good to eat much honey: so for men to search their own glory is not glory.

28 He that hath no rule over his own spirit is like a city that is broken down, and without walls.

Chapter 26

1 As snow in summer, and as rain in harvest, so honour is not seemly for a fool.

2 As the bird by wandering, as the swallow by flying, so the curse causeless shall not come.

3 A whip for the horse, a bridle for the ass, and a rod for the fool's back.

4 Answer not a fool according to his folly, lest thou also be like unto him.

5 Answer a fool according to his folly, lest he be wise in his own conceit.

6 He that sendeth a message by the hand of a fool cutteth off the feet, and drinketh damage.

7 The legs of the lame are not equal: so is a parable in the mouth of fools.

8 As he that bindeth a stone in a sling, so is he that giveth honour to a fool.

9 As a thorn goeth up into the hand of a drunkard, so is a parable in the mouths of fools.

10 The great God that formed all things both rewardeth the fool, and rewardeth transgressors.

11 As a dog returneth to his vomit, so a fool returneth to his folly.

12 Seest thou a man wise in his own conceit? there is more hope of a fool than of him.

13 The slothful man saith, There is a lion in the way; a lion is in the streets.

14 As the door turneth upon his hinges, so doth the slothful upon his bed.

15 The slothful hideth his hand in his bosom; it grieveth him to bring it again to his mouth.

16 The sluggard is wiser in his own conceit than seven men that can render a reason.

17 He that passeth by, and meddleth with strife belonging not to him, is like one that taketh a dog by the ears.

18 As a mad man who casteth firebrands, arrows, and death,

19 So is the man that deceiveth his neighbour, and saith, Am not I in sport?

20 Where no wood is, there the fire goeth out: so where there is no talebearer, the strife ceaseth.

21 As coals are to burning coals, and wood to fire; so is a contentious man to kindle strife.

22 The words of a talebearer are as wounds, and they go down into the innermost parts of the belly.

23 Burning lips and a wicked heart are like a potsherd covered with silver dross.

24 He that hateth dissembleth with his lips, and layeth up deceit within him;

25 When he speaketh fair, believe him not: for there are seven abominations in his heart.

26 Whose hatred is covered by deceit, his wickedness shall be shewed before the whole congregation.

27 Whoso diggeth a pit shall fall therein: and he that rolleth a stone, it will return upon him.

28 A lying tongue hateth those that are afflicted by it; and a flattering mouth worketh ruin.

Chapter 27

1 Boast not thyself of to morrow; for thou knowest not what a day may bring forth.

2 Let another man praise thee, and not thine own mouth; a stranger, and not thine own lips.

3 A stone is heavy, and the sand weighty; but a fool's wrath is heavier than them both.

4 Wrath is cruel, and anger is outrageous; but who is able to stand before envy?

5 Open rebuke is better than secret love.

6 Faithful are the wounds of a friend; but the kisses of an enemy are deceitful.

7 The full soul loatheth an honeycomb; but to the hungry soul every bitter thing is sweet.

8 As a bird that wandereth from her nest, so is a man that wandereth from his place.

9 Ointment and perfume rejoice the heart: so doth the sweetness of a man's friend by hearty counsel.

10 Thine own friend, and thy father's friend, forsake not; neither go into thy brother's house in the day of thy calamity: for better is a neighbour that is near than a brother far off.

11 My son, be wise, and make my heart glad, that I may answer him that reproacheth me.

12 A prudent man foreseeth the evil, and hideth himself; but the simple pass on, and are punished.

13 Take his garment that is surety for a stranger, and take a pledge of him for a strange woman.

14 He that blesseth his friend with a loud voice, rising early in the morning, it shall be counted a curse to him.

15 A continual dropping in a very rainy day and a contentious woman are alike.

16 Whosoever hideth her hideth the wind, and the ointment of his right hand, which bewrayeth itself.

17 Iron sharpeneth iron; so a man sharpeneth the countenance of his friend.

18 Whoso keepeth the fig tree shall eat the fruit thereof: so he that waiteth on his master shall be honoured.

19 As in water face answereth to face, so the heart of man to man.

20 Hell and destruction are never full; so the eyes of man are never satisfied.

21 As the fining pot for silver, and the furnace for gold; so is a man to his praise.

22 Though thou shouldest bray a fool in a mortar among wheat with a pestle, yet will not his foolishness depart from him.

23 Be thou diligent to know the state of thy flocks, and look well to thy herds.

24 For riches are not for ever: and doth the crown endure to every generation?

25 The hay appeareth, and the tender grass sheweth itself, and herbs of the mountains are gathered.

26 The lambs are for thy clothing, and the goats are the price of the field.

27 And thou shalt have goats' milk enough for thy food, for the food of thy household, and for the maintenance for thy maidens.

Chapter 28

1 The wicked flee when no man pursueth: but the righteous are bold as a lion.

2 For the transgression of a land many are the princes thereof: but by a man of understanding and knowledge the state thereof shall be prolonged.

3 A poor man that oppresseth the poor is like a sweeping rain which leaveth no food.

4 They that forsake the law praise the wicked: but such as keep the law contend with them.

5 Evil men understand not judgment: but they that seek the LORD understand all things.

6 Better is the poor that walketh in his uprightness, than he that is perverse in his ways, though he be rich.

7 Whoso keepeth the law is a wise son: but he that is a companion of riotous men shameth his father.

8 He that by usury and unjust gain increaseth his substance, he shall gather it for him that will pity the poor.

9 He that turneth away his ear from hearing the law, even his prayer shall be abomination.

10 Whoso causeth the righteous to go astray in an evil way, he shall fall himself into his own pit: but the upright shall have good things in possession.

11 The rich man is wise in his own conceit; but the poor that hath understanding searcheth him out.

12 When righteous men do rejoice, there is great glory: but when the wicked rise, a man is hidden.

13 He that covereth his sins shall not prosper: but whoso confesseth and forsaketh them shall have mercy.

14 Happy is the man that feareth alway: but he that hardeneth his heart shall fall into mischief.

15 As a roaring lion, and a ranging bear; so is a wicked ruler over the poor people.

16 The prince that wanteth understanding is also a great oppressor: but he that hateth covetousness shall prolong his days.

17 A man that doeth violence to the blood of any person shall flee to the pit; let no man stay him.

18 Whoso walketh uprightly shall be saved: but he that is perverse in his ways shall fall at once.

19 He that tilleth his land shall have plenty of bread: but he that followeth after vain persons shall have poverty enough.

20 A faithful man shall abound with blessings: but he that maketh haste to be rich shall not be innocent.

21 To have respect of persons is not good: for for a piece of bread that man will transgress.

22 He that hasteth to be rich hath an evil eye, and considereth not that poverty shall come upon him.

23 He that rebuketh a man afterwards shall find more favour than he that flattereth with the tongue.

24 Whoso robbeth his father or his mother, and saith, It is no transgression; the same is the companion of a destroyer.

25 He that is of a proud heart stirreth up strife: but he that putteth his trust in the LORD shall be made fat.

26 He that trusteth in his own heart is a fool: but whoso walketh wisely, he shall be delivered.

27 He that giveth unto the poor shall not lack: but he that hideth his eyes shall have many a curse.

28 When the wicked rise, men hide themselves: but when they perish, the righteous increase.

Chapter 29

1 He, that being often reproved hardeneth his neck, shall suddenly be destroyed, and that without remedy.

2 When the righteous are in authority, the people rejoice: but when the wicked beareth rule, the people mourn.

3 Whoso loveth wisdom rejoiceth his father: but he that keepeth company with harlots spendeth his substance.

4 The king by judgment establisheth the land: but he that receiveth gifts overthroweth it.

5 A man that flattereth his neighbour spreadeth a net for his feet.

6 In the transgression of an evil man there is a snare: but the righteous doth sing and rejoice.

7 The righteous considereth the cause of the poor: but the wicked regardeth not to know it.

8 Scornful men bring a city into a snare: but wise men turn away wrath.

9 If a wise man contendeth with a foolish man, whether he rage or laugh, there is no rest.

10 The bloodthirsty hate the upright: but the just seek his soul.

11 A fool uttereth all his mind: but a wise man keepeth it in till afterwards.

12 If a ruler hearken to lies, all his servants are wicked.

13 The poor and the deceitful man meet together: the LORD lighteneth both their eyes.

14 The king that faithfully judgeth the poor, his throne shall be established for ever.

15 The rod and reproof give wisdom: but a child left to himself bringeth his mother to shame.

16 When the wicked are multiplied, transgression increaseth: but the righteous shall see their fall.

17 Correct thy son, and he shall give thee rest; yea, he shall give delight unto thy soul.

18 Where there is no vision, the people perish: but he that keepeth the law, happy is he.

19 A servant will not be corrected by words: for though he understand he will not answer.

20 Seest thou a man that is hasty in his words? there is more hope of a fool than of him.

21 He that delicately bringeth up his servant from a child shall have him become his son at the length.

22 An angry man stirreth up strife, and a furious man aboundeth in transgression.

23 A man's pride shall bring him low: but honour shall uphold the humble in spirit.

24 Whoso is partner with a thief hateth his own soul: he heareth cursing, and bewrayeth it not.

25 The fear of man bringeth a snare: but whoso putteth his trust in the LORD shall be safe.

26 Many seek the ruler's favour; but every man's judgment cometh from the LORD.

27 An unjust man is an abomination to the just: and he that is upright in the way is abomination to the wicked.

Chapter 30

1 The words of Agur the son of Jakeh, even the prophecy: the man spake unto Ithiel, even unto Ithiel and Ucal,

2 Surely I am more brutish than any man, and have not the understanding of a man.

3 I neither learned wisdom, nor have the knowledge of the holy.

4 Who hath ascended up into heaven, or descended? who hath gathered the wind in his fists? who hath bound the waters in a garment? who hath established all the ends of the earth? what is his name, and what is his son's name, if thou canst tell?

5 Every word of God is pure: he is a shield unto them that put their trust in him.

6 Add thou not unto his words, lest he reprove thee, and thou be found a liar.

7 Two things have I required of thee; deny me them not before I die:

8 Remove far from me vanity and lies: give me neither poverty nor riches; feed me with food convenient for me:

9 Lest I be full, and deny thee, and say, Who is the LORD? or lest I be poor, and steal, and take the name of my God in vain.

10 Accuse not a servant unto his master, lest he curse thee, and thou be found guilty.

11 There is a generation that curseth their father, and doth not bless their mother.

12 There is a generation that are pure in their own eyes, and yet is not washed from their filthiness.

13 There is a generation, O how lofty are their eyes! and their eyelids are lifted up.

14 There is a generation, whose teeth are as swords, and their jaw teeth as knives, to devour the poor from off the earth, and the needy from among men.

15 The horseleach hath two daughters, crying, Give, give. There are three things that are never satisfied, yea, four things say not, It is enough:

16 The grave; and the barren womb; the earth that is not filled with water; and the fire that saith not, It is enough.

17 The eye that mocketh at his father, and despiseth to obey his mother, the ravens of the valley shall pick it out, and the young eagles shall eat it.

18 There be three things which are too wonderful for me, yea, four which I know not:

19 The way of an eagle in the air; the way of a serpent upon a rock; the way of a ship in the midst of the sea; and the way of a man with a maid.

20 Such is the way of an adulterous woman; she eateth, and wipeth her mouth, and saith, I have done no wickedness.

21 For three things the earth is disquieted, and for four which it cannot bear:

22 For a servant when he reigneth; and a fool when he is filled with meat;

23 For an odious woman when she is married; and an handmaid that is heir to her mistress.

24 There be four things which are little upon the earth, but they are exceeding wise:

25 The ants are a people not strong, yet they prepare their meat in the summer;

26 The conies are but a feeble folk, yet make they their houses in the rocks;

27 The locusts have no king, yet go they forth all of them by bands;

28 The spider taketh hold with her hands, and is in kings' palaces.

29 There be three things which go well, yea, four are comely in going:

30 A lion which is strongest among beasts, and turneth not away for any;

31 A greyhound; an he goat also; and a king, against whom there is no rising up.

32 If thou hast done foolishly in lifting up thyself, or if thou hast thought evil, lay thine hand upon thy mouth.

33 Surely the churning of milk bringeth forth butter, and the wringing of the nose bringeth forth blood: so the forcing of wrath bringeth forth strife.

Chapter 31

1 The words of king Lemuel, the prophecy that his mother taught him.

2 What, my son? and what, the son of my womb? and what, the son of my vows? 3 Give not thy strength unto women, nor thy ways to that which destroyeth kings.

4 It is not for kings, O Lemuel, it is not for kings to drink wine; nor for princes strong drink:

5 Lest they drink, and forget the law, and pervert the judgment of any of the afflicted.

6 Give strong drink unto him that is ready to perish, and wine unto those that be of heavy hearts.

7 Let him drink, and forget his poverty, and remember his misery no more.

8 Open thy mouth for the dumb in the cause of all such as are appointed to destruction.

9 Open thy mouth, judge righteously, and plead the cause of the poor and needy.

10 Who can find a virtuous woman? for her price is far above rubies.

11 The heart of her husband doth safely trust in her, so that he shall have no need of spoil.

12 She will do him good and not evil all the days of her life.

13 She seeketh wool, and flax, and worketh willingly with her hands.

14 She is like the merchants' ships; she bringeth her food from afar.

15 She riseth also while it is yet night, and giveth meat to her household, and a portion to her maidens.

16 She considereth a field, and buyeth it: with the fruit of her hands she planteth a vineyard.

17 She girdeth her loins with strength, and strengtheneth her arms.

18 She perceiveth that her merchandise is good: her candle goeth not out by night.

19 She layeth her hands to the spindle, and her hands hold the distaff.

20 She stretcheth out her hand to the poor; yea, she reacheth forth her hands to the needy.

21 She is not afraid of the snow for her household: for all her household are clothed with scarlet.

22 She maketh herself coverings of tapestry; her clothing is silk and purple.

23 Her husband is known in the gates, when he sitteth among the elders of the land.

24 She maketh fine linen, and selleth it; and delivereth girdles unto the merchant.

25 Strength and honour are her clothing; and she shall rejoice in time to come.

26 She openeth her mouth with wisdom; and in her tongue is the law of kindness.

27 She looketh well to the ways of her household, and eateth not the bread of idleness.

28 Her children arise up, and call her blessed; her husband also, and he praiseth her.

29 Many daughters have done virtuously, but thou excellest them all.

30 Favour is deceitful, and beauty is vain: but a woman that feareth the LORD, she shall be praised.

31 Give her of the fruit of her hands; and let her own works praise her in the gates.

Ecclesiastes

or

The Preacher
(King James Version)

Chapter 1

1 The words of the Preacher, the son of David, king in Jerusalem.

2 Vanity of vanities, saith the Preacher, vanity of vanities; all is vanity.

3 What profit hath a man of all his labour which he taketh under the sun?

4 One generation passeth away, and another generation cometh: but the earth abideth for ever.

5 The sun also ariseth, and the sun goeth down, and hasteth to his place where he arose.

6 The wind goeth toward the south, and turneth about unto the north; it whirleth about continually, and the wind returneth again according to his circuits.

7 All the rivers run into the sea; yet the sea is not full; unto the place from whence the rivers come, thither they return again.

8 All things are full of labour; man cannot utter it: the eye is not satisfied with seeing, nor the ear filled with hearing.

9 The thing that hath been, it is that which shall be; and that which is done is that which shall be done: and there is no new thing under the sun.

10 Is there any thing whereof it may be said, See, this is new? it hath been already of old time, which was before us.

11 There is no remembrance of former things; neither shall there be any remembrance of things that are to come with those that shall come after.

12 I the Preacher was king over Israel in Jerusalem.

13 And I gave my heart to seek and search out by wisdom concerning all things that are done under heaven: this sore travail hath God given to the sons of man to be exercised therewith.

14 I have seen all the works that are done under the sun; and, behold, all is vanity and vexation of spirit.

15 That which is crooked cannot be made straight: and that which is wanting cannot be numbered.

16 I communed with mine own heart, saying, Lo, I am come to great estate, and have gotten more wisdom than all they that have been before me in Jerusalem: yea, my heart had great experience of wisdom and knowledge.

17 And I gave my heart to know wisdom, and to know madness and folly: I perceived that this also is vexation of spirit.

18 For in much wisdom is much grief: and he that increaseth knowledge increaseth sorrow.

Chapter 2

1 I said in mine heart, Go to now, I will prove thee with mirth, therefore enjoy pleasure: and, behold, this also is vanity.

2 I said of laughter, It is mad: and of mirth, What doeth it?

3 I sought in mine heart to give myself unto wine, yet acquainting mine heart with wisdom; and to lay hold on folly, till I might see what was that good for the sons of men, which they should do under the heaven all the days of their life.

4 I made me great works; I builded me houses; I planted me vineyards:

5 I made me gardens and orchards, and I planted trees in them of all kind of fruits:

6 I made me pools of water, to water therewith the wood that bringeth forth trees:

7 I got me servants and maidens, and had servants born in my house; also I had great possessions of great and small cattle above all that were in Jerusalem before me:

8 I gathered me also silver and gold, and the peculiar treasure of kings and of the provinces: I gat me men singers and women singers, and the delights of the sons of men, as musical instruments, and that of all sorts.

9 So I was great, and increased more than all that were before me in Jerusalem: also my wisdom remained with me.

10 And whatsoever mine eyes desired I kept not from them, I withheld not my heart from any joy; for my heart rejoiced in all my labour: and this was my portion of all my labour.

11 Then I looked on all the works that my hands had wrought, and on the labour that I had laboured to do: and, behold, all was vanity and vexation of spirit, and there was no profit under the sun.

12 And I turned myself to behold wisdom, and madness, and folly: for what can the man do that cometh after the king? even that which hath been already done.

13 Then I saw that wisdom excelleth folly, as far as light excelleth darkness.

14 The wise man's eyes are in his head; but the fool walketh in darkness: and I myself perceived also that one event happeneth to them all.

15 Then said I in my heart, As it happeneth to the fool, so it happeneth even to me; and why was I then more wise? Then I said in my heart, that this also is vanity.

16 For there is no remembrance of the wise more than of the fool for ever; seeing that which now is in the days to come shall all be forgotten.

And how dieth the wise man? as the fool.

17 Therefore I hated life; because the work that is wrought under the sun is grievous unto me: for all is vanity and vexation of spirit.

18 Yea, I hated all my labour which I had taken under the sun: because I should leave it unto the man that shall be after me.

19 And who knoweth whether he shall be a wise man or a fool? yet shall he have rule over all my labour wherein I have laboured, and wherein I have shewed myself wise under the sun. This is also vanity.

20 Therefore I went about to cause my heart to despair of all the labour which I took under the sun.

21 For there is a man whose labour is in wisdom, and in knowledge, and in equity; yet to a man that hath not laboured therein shall he leave it for his portion. This also is vanity and a great evil.

22 For what hath man of all his labour, and of the vexation of his heart, wherein he hath laboured under the sun?

23 For all his days are sorrows, and his travail grief; yea, his heart taketh not rest in the night. This is also vanity.

24 There is nothing better for a man, than that he should eat and drink, and that he should make his soul enjoy good in his labour. This also I saw, that it was from the hand of God.

25 For who can eat, or who else can hasten hereunto, more than I?

26 For God giveth to a man that is good in his sight wisdom, and knowledge, and joy: but to the sinner he giveth travail, to gather and to heap up, that he may give to him that is good before God. This also is vanity and vexation of spirit.

Chapter 3

1 To every thing there is a season, and a time to every purpose under the heaven:

2 A time to be born, and a time to die; a time to plant, and a time to pluck up that which is planted;

3 A time to kill, and a time to heal; a time to break down, and a time to build up;

4 A time to weep, and a time to laugh; a time to mourn, and a time to dance;

5 A time to cast away stones, and a time to gather stones together; a time to embrace, and a time to refrain from embracing;

6 A time to get, and a time to lose; a time to keep, and a time to cast away;

7 A time to rend, and a time to sew; a time to keep silence, and a time to speak;

8 A time to love, and a time to hate; a time of war, and a time of peace.

9 What profit hath he that worketh in that wherein he laboureth?

10 I have seen the travail, which God hath given to the sons of men to be exercised in it.

11 He hath made every thing beautiful in his time: also he hath set the world in their heart, so that no man can find out the work that God maketh from the beginning to the end.

12 I know that there is no good in them, but for a man to rejoice, and to do good in his life.

13 And also that every man should eat and drink, and enjoy the good of all his labour, it is the gift of God.

14 I know that, whatsoever God doeth, it shall be for ever: nothing can be put to it, nor any thing taken from it: and God doeth it, that men should fear before him.

15 That which hath been is now; and that which is to be hath already been; and God requireth that which is past.

16 And moreover I saw under the sun the place of judgment, that wickedness was there; and the place of righteousness, that iniquity was there.

17 I said in mine heart, God shall judge the righteous and the wicked: for there is a time there for every purpose and for every work.

18 I said in mine heart concerning the estate of the sons of men, that God might manifest them, and that they might see that they themselves are beasts.

19 For that which befalleth the sons of men befalleth beasts; even one thing befalleth them: as the one dieth, so dieth the other; yea, they have all one breath; so that a man hath no preeminence above a beast: for all is vanity.

20 All go unto one place; all are of the dust, and all turn to dust again.

21 Who knoweth the spirit of man that goeth upward, and the spirit of the beast that goeth downward to the earth?

22 Wherefore I perceive that there is nothing better, than that a man should rejoice in his own works; for that is his portion: for who shall bring him to see what shall be after him?

Chapter 4

1 So I returned, and considered all the oppressions that are done under the sun: and behold the tears of such as were oppressed, and they had no comforter; and on the side of their oppressors there was power; but they had no comforter.

2 Wherefore I praised the dead which are already dead more than the living which are yet alive.

3 Yea, better is he than both they, which hath not yet been, who hath not seen the evil work that is done under the sun.

4 Again, I considered all travail, and every right work, that for this a man is envied of his neighbour. This is also vanity and vexation of spirit.

5 The fool foldeth his hands together, and eateth his own flesh.

6 Better is an handful with quietness, than both the hands full with travail and vexation of spirit.

7 Then I returned, and I saw vanity under the sun.

8 There is one alone, and there is not a second; yea, he hath neither child nor brother: yet is there no end of all his labour; neither is his eye satisfied with riches; neither saith he, For whom do I labour, and bereave my soul of good? This is also vanity, yea, it is a sore travail.

9 Two are better than one; because they have a good reward for their labour.

10 For if they fall, the one will lift up his fellow: but woe to him that is alone when he falleth; for he hath not another to help him up.

11 Again, if two lie together, then they have heat: but how can one be warm alone?

12 And if one prevail against him, two shall withstand him; and a threefold cord is not quickly broken.

13 Better is a poor and a wise child than an old and foolish king, who will no more be admonished.

14 For out of prison he cometh to reign; whereas also he that is born in his kingdom becometh poor.

15 I considered all the living which walk under the sun, with the second child that shall stand up in his stead.

16 There is no end of all the people, even of all that have been before them: they also that come after shall not rejoice in him. Surely this also is vanity and vexation of spirit.

Chapter 5

1 Keep thy foot when thou goest to the house of God, and be more ready to hear, than to give the sacrifice of fools: for they consider not that they do evil.

2 Be not rash with thy mouth, and let not thine heart be hasty to utter any thing before God: for God is in heaven, and thou upon earth: therefore let thy words be few.

3 For a dream cometh through the multitude of business; and a fool's voice is known by multitude of words.

4 When thou vowest a vow unto God, defer not to pay it; for he hath no pleasure in fools: pay that which thou hast vowed.

5 Better is it that thou shouldest not vow, than that thou shouldest vow and not pay.

6 Suffer not thy mouth to cause thy flesh to sin; neither say thou before the angel, that it was an error: wherefore should God be angry at thy voice, and destroy the work of thine hands?

7 For in the multitude of dreams and many words there are also divers vanities: but fear thou God.

8 If thou seest the oppression of the poor, and violent perverting of judgment and justice in a province, marvel not at the matter: for he that is higher than the highest regardeth; and there be higher than they.

9 Moreover the profit of the earth is for all: the king himself is served by the field.

10 He that loveth silver shall not be satisfied with silver; nor he that loveth abundance with increase: this is also vanity.

11 When goods increase, they are increased that eat them: and what good is there to the owners thereof, saving the beholding of them with their eyes?

12 The sleep of a labouring man is sweet, whether he eat little or much: but the abundance of the rich will not suffer him to sleep.

13 There is a sore evil which I have seen under the sun, namely, riches kept for the owners thereof to their hurt.

14 But those riches perish by evil travail: and he begetteth a son, and there is nothing in his hand.

15 As he came forth of his mother's womb, naked shall he return to go as he came, and shall take nothing of his labour, which he may carry away in his hand.

16 And this also is a sore evil, that in all points as he came, so shall he go: and what profit hath he that hath laboured for the wind?

17 All his days also he eateth in darkness, and he hath much sorrow and wrath with his sickness.

18 Behold that which I have seen: it is good and comely for one to eat and to drink, and to enjoy the good of all his labour that he taketh under the sun all the days of his life, which God giveth him: for it is his portion.

19 Every man also to whom God hath given riches and wealth, and hath given him power to eat thereof, and to take his portion, and to rejoice in his labour; this is the gift of God.

20 For he shall not much remember the days of his life; because God answereth him in the joy of his heart.

Chapter 6

1 There is an evil which I have seen under the sun, and it is common among men:

2 A man to whom God hath given riches, wealth, and honour, so that he wanteth nothing for his soul of all that he desireth, yet God giveth him not power to eat thereof, but a stranger eateth it: this is vanity, and it is an evil disease.

3 If a man beget an hundred children, and live many years, so that the days of his years be many, and his soul be not filled with good, and also that he have no burial; I say, that an untimely birth is better than he.

4 For he cometh in with vanity, and departeth in darkness, and his name shall be covered with darkness.

5 Moreover he hath not seen the sun, nor known any thing: this hath more rest than the other.

6 Yea, though he live a thousand years twice told, yet hath he seen no good: do not all go to one place?

7 All the labour of man is for his mouth, and yet the appetite is not filled.

8 For what hath the wise more than the fool? what hath the poor, that knoweth to walk before the living?

9 Better is the sight of the eyes than the wandering of the desire: this is also vanity and vexation of spirit.

10 That which hath been is named already, and it is known that it is man: neither may he contend with him that is mightier than he.

11 Seeing there be many things that increase vanity, what is man the better?

12 For who knoweth what is good for man in this life, all the days of his vain life which he spendeth as a shadow? for who can tell a man what shall be after him under the sun?

Chapter 7

1 A good name is better than precious ointment; and the day of death than the day of one's birth.

2 It is better to go to the house of mourning, than to go to the house of feasting: for that is the end of all men; and the living will lay it to his heart.

3 Sorrow is better than laughter: for by the sadness of the countenance the heart is made better.

4 The heart of the wise is in the house of mourning; but the heart of fools is in the house of mirth.

5 It is better to hear the rebuke of the wise, than for a man to hear the song of fools.

6 For as the crackling of thorns under a pot, so is the laughter of the fool: this also is vanity.

7 Surely oppression maketh a wise man mad; and a gift destroyeth the heart.

8 Better is the end of a thing than the beginning thereof: and the patient in spirit is better than the proud in spirit.

9 Be not hasty in thy spirit to be angry: for anger resteth in the bosom of fools.

10 Say not thou, What is the cause that the former days were better than these? for thou dost not enquire wisely concerning this.

11 Wisdom is good with an inheritance: and by it there is profit to them that see the sun.

12 For wisdom is a defence, and money is a defence: but the excellency of knowledge is, that wisdom giveth life to them that have it.

13 Consider the work of God: for who can make that straight, which he hath made crooked?

14 In the day of prosperity be joyful, but in the day of adversity consider: God also hath set the one over against the other, to the end that man should find nothing after him.

15 All things have I seen in the days of my vanity: there is a just man that perisheth in his righteousness, and there is a wicked man that prolongeth his life in his wickedness.

16 Be not righteous over much; neither make thyself over wise: why shouldest thou destroy thyself?

17 Be not over much wicked, neither be thou foolish: why shouldest thou die before thy time?

18 It is good that thou shouldest take hold of this; yea, also from this withdraw not thine hand: for he that feareth God shall come forth of them all.

19 Wisdom strengtheneth the wise more than ten mighty men which are in the city.

20 For there is not a just man upon earth, that doeth good, and sinneth not.

21 Also take no heed unto all words that are spoken; lest thou hear thy servant curse thee:

22 For oftentimes also thine own heart knoweth that thou thyself likewise hast cursed others.

23 All this have I proved by wisdom: I said, I will be wise; but it was far from me.

24 That which is far off, and exceeding deep, who can find it out?

25 I applied mine heart to know, and to search, and to seek out wisdom, and the reason of things, and to know the wickedness of folly, even of foolishness and madness:

26 And I find more bitter than death the woman, whose heart is snares and nets, and her hands as bands: whoso pleaseth God shall escape from her; but the sinner shall be taken by her.

27 Behold, this have I found, saith the preacher, counting one by one, to find out the account:

28 Which yet my soul seeketh, but I find not: one man among a thousand have I found; but a woman among all those have I not found.

29 Lo, this only have I found, that God hath made man upright; but they have sought out many inventions.

Chapter 8

1 Who is as the wise man? and who knoweth the interpretation of a thing? a man's wisdom maketh his face to shine, and the boldness of his face shall be changed.

2 I counsel thee to keep the king's commandment, and that in regard of the oath of God.

3 Be not hasty to go out of his sight: stand not in an evil thing; for he doeth whatsoever pleaseth him.

4 Where the word of a king is, there is power: and who may say unto him, What doest thou?

5 Whoso keepeth the commandment shall feel no evil thing: and a wise man's heart discerneth both time and judgment.

6 Because to every purpose there is time and judgment, therefore the misery of man is great upon him.

7 For he knoweth not that which shall be: for who can tell him when it shall be?

8 There is no man that hath power over the spirit to retain the spirit; neither hath he power in the day of death: and there is no discharge in that war; neither shall wickedness deliver those that are given to it.

9 All this have I seen, and applied my heart unto every work that is done under the sun: there is a time wherein one man ruleth over another to his own hurt.

10 And so I saw the wicked buried, who had come and gone from the place of the holy, and they were forgotten in the city where they had so done: this is also vanity.

11 Because sentence against an evil work is not executed speedily, therefore the heart of the sons of men is fully set in them to do evil.

12 Though a sinner do evil an hundred times, and his days be prolonged, yet surely I know that it shall be well with them that fear God, which fear before him:

13 But it shall not be well with the wicked, neither shall he prolong his days, which are as a shadow; because he feareth not before God.

14 There is a vanity which is done upon the earth; that there be just men, unto whom it happeneth according to the work of the wicked; again, there be wicked men, to whom it happeneth according to the work of the righteous: I said that this also is vanity.

15 Then I commended mirth, because a man hath no better thing under the sun, than to eat, and to drink, and to be merry: for that shall abide with him of his labour the days of his life, which God giveth him under the sun.

16 When I applied mine heart to know wisdom, and to see the business that is done upon the earth: (for also there is that neither day nor night seeth sleep with his eyes:)

17 Then I beheld all the work of God, that a man cannot find out the work that is done under the sun: because though a man labour to

seek it out, yet he shall not find it; yea farther; though a wise man think to know it, yet shall he not be able to find it.

Chapter 9

1 For all this I considered in my heart even to declare all this, that the righteous, and the wise, and their works, are in the hand of God: no man knoweth either love or hatred by all that is before them.

2 All things come alike to all: there is one event to the righteous, and to the wicked; to the good and to the clean, and to the unclean; to him that sacrificeth, and to him that sacrificeth not: as is the good, so is the sinner; and he that sweareth, as he that feareth an oath.

3 This is an evil among all things that are done under the sun, that there is one event unto all: yea, also the heart of the sons of men is full of evil, and madness is in their heart while they live, and after that they go to the dead.

4 For to him that is joined to all the living there is hope: for a living dog is better than a dead lion.

5 For the living know that they shall die: but the dead know not any thing, neither have they any more a reward; for the memory of them is forgotten.

6 Also their love, and their hatred, and their envy, is now perished; neither have they any more a portion for ever in any thing that is done under the sun.

7 Go thy way, eat thy bread with joy, and drink thy wine with a merry heart; for God now accepteth thy works.

8 Let thy garments be always white; and let thy head lack no ointment.

9 Live joyfully with the wife whom thou lovest all the days of the life of thy vanity, which he hath given thee under the sun, all the days of thy vanity: for that is thy portion in this life, and in thy labour which thou takest under the sun.

10 Whatsoever thy hand findeth to do, do it with thy might; for there is no work, nor device, nor knowledge, nor wisdom, in the grave, whither thou goest.

11 I returned, and saw under the sun, that the race is not to the swift, nor the battle to the strong, neither yet bread to the wise, nor yet riches to men of understanding, nor yet favour to men of skill; but time and chance happeneth to them all.

12 For man also knoweth not his time: as the fishes that are taken in an evil net, and as the birds that are caught in the snare; so are the sons of men snared in an evil time, when it falleth suddenly upon them.

13 This wisdom have I seen also under the sun, and it seemed great unto me:

14 There was a little city, and few men within it; and there came a great king against it, and besieged it, and built great bulwarks against it:

15 Now there was found in it a poor wise man, and he by his wisdom delivered the city; yet no man remembered that same poor man.

16 Then said I, Wisdom is better than strength: nevertheless the poor man's wisdom is despised, and his words are not heard.

17 The words of wise men are heard in quiet more than the cry of him that ruleth among fools.

18 Wisdom is better than weapons of war: but one sinner destroyeth much good.

Chapter 10

1 Dead flies cause the ointment of the apothecary to send forth a stinking savour: so doth a little folly him that is in reputation for wisdom and honour.

2 A wise man's heart is at his right hand; but a fool's heart at his left.

3 Yea also, when he that is a fool walketh by the way, his wisdom faileth him, and he saith to every one that he is a fool.

4 If the spirit of the ruler rise up against thee, leave not thy place; for yielding pacifieth great offences.

5 There is an evil which I have seen under the sun, as an error which proceedeth from the ruler:

6 Folly is set in great dignity, and the rich sit in low place.

7 I have seen servants upon horses, and princes walking as servants upon the earth.

8 He that diggeth a pit shall fall into it; and whoso breaketh an hedge, a serpent shall bite him.

9 Whoso removeth stones shall be hurt therewith; and he that cleaveth wood shall be endangered thereby.

10 If the iron be blunt, and he do not whet the edge, then must he put to more strength: but wisdom is profitable to direct.

11 Surely the serpent will bite without enchantment; and a babbler is no better.

12 The words of a wise man's mouth are gracious; but the lips of a fool will swallow up himself.

13 The beginning of the words of his mouth is foolishness: and the end of his talk is mischievous madness.

14 A fool also is full of words: a man cannot tell what shall be; and what shall be after him, who can tell him?

15 The labour of the foolish wearieth every one of them, because he knoweth not how to go to the city.

16 Woe to thee, O land, when thy king is a child, and thy princes eat in the morning!

17 Blessed art thou, O land, when thy king is the son of nobles, and thy princes eat in due season, for strength, and not for drunkenness!

18 By much slothfulness the building decayeth; and through idleness of the hands the house droppeth through.

19 A feast is made for laughter, and wine maketh merry: but money answereth all things.

20 Curse not the king, no not in thy thought; and curse not the rich in thy bedchamber: for a bird of the air shall carry the voice, and that which hath wings shall tell the matter.

Chapter 11

1 Cast thy bread upon the waters: for thou shalt find it after many days.

2 Give a portion to seven, and also to eight; for thou knowest not what evil shall be upon the earth.

3 If the clouds be full of rain, they empty themselves upon the earth: and if the tree fall toward the south, or toward the north, in the place where the tree falleth, there it shall be.

4 He that observeth the wind shall not sow; and he that regardeth the clouds shall not reap.

5 As thou knowest not what is the way of the spirit, nor how the bones do grow in the womb of her that is with child: even so thou knowest not the works of God who maketh all.

6 In the morning sow thy seed, and in the evening withhold not thine hand: for thou knowest not whether shall prosper, either this or that, or whether they both shall be alike good.

7 Truly the light is sweet, and a pleasant thing it is for the eyes to behold the sun:

8 But if a man live many years, and rejoice in them all; yet let him remember the days of darkness; for they shall be many. All that cometh is vanity.

9 Rejoice, O young man, in thy youth; and let thy heart cheer thee in the days of thy youth, and walk in the ways of thine heart, and in the sight of thine eyes: but know thou, that for all these things God will bring thee into judgment.

10 Therefore remove sorrow from thy heart, and put away evil from thy flesh: for childhood and youth are vanity.

Chapter 12

1 Remember now thy Creator in the days of thy youth, while the evil days come not, nor the years draw nigh, when thou shalt say, I have no pleasure in them;

2 While the sun, or the light, or the moon, or the stars, be not darkened, nor the clouds return after the rain:

3 In the day when the keepers of the house shall tremble, and the strong men shall bow themselves, and the grinders cease because they are few, and those that look out of the windows be darkened,

4 And the doors shall be shut in the streets, when the sound of the grinding is low, and he shall rise up at the voice of the bird, and all the daughters of musick shall be brought low;

5 Also when they shall be afraid of that which is high, and fears shall be in the way, and the almond tree shall flourish, and the grasshopper shall be a burden, and desire shall fail: because man goeth to his long home, and the mourners go about the streets:

6 Or ever the silver cord be loosed, or the golden bowl be broken, or the pitcher be broken at the fountain, or the wheel broken at the cistern.

7 Then shall the dust return to the earth as it was: and the spirit shall return unto God who gave it.

8 Vanity of vanities, saith the preacher; all is vanity.

9 And moreover, because the preacher was wise, he still taught the people knowledge; yea, he gave good heed, and sought out, and set in order many proverbs.

10 The preacher sought to find out acceptable words: and that which was written was upright, even words of truth.

11 The words of the wise are as goads, and as nails fastened by the masters of assemblies, which are given from one shepherd.

12 And further, by these, my son, be admonished: of making many books there is no end; and much study is a weariness of the flesh.

13 Let us hear the conclusion of the whole matter: Fear God, and keep his commandments: for this is the whole duty of man.

14 For God shall bring every work into judgment, with every secret thing, whether it be good, or whether it be evil.

The Wisdom of Solomon

(Vulgate)

Chapter 1

1 Love righteousness, ye that be judges of the earth: think of the Lord with a good (heart,) and in simplicity of heart seek him.

2 For he will be found of them that tempt him not; and sheweth himself unto such as do not distrust him.

3 For froward thoughts separate from God: and his power, when it is tried, reproveth the unwise.

4 For into a malicious soul wisdom shall not enter; nor dwell in the body that is subject unto sin.

5 For the holy spirit of discipline will flee deceit, and remove from thoughts that are without understanding, and will not abide when unrighteousness cometh in.

6 For wisdom is a loving spirit; and will not acquit a blasphemer of his words: for God is witness of his reins, and a true beholder of his heart, and a hearer of his tongue.

7 For the Spirit of the Lord filleth the world: and that which containeth all things hath knowledge of the voice.

8 Therefore he that speaketh unrighteous things cannot be hid: neither shall vengeance, when it punisheth, pass by him.

9 For inquisition shall be made into the counsels of the ungodly: and the sound of his words shall come unto the Lord for the manifestation of his wicked deeds.

10 For the ear of jealousy heareth all things: and the noise of murmurings is not hid.

11 Therefore beware of murmuring, which is unprofitable; and refrain your tongue from backbiting: for there is no word so secret, that shall go for nought: and the mouth that belieth slayeth the soul.

12 Seek not death in the error of your life: and pull not upon yourselves destruction with the works of your hands.

13 For God made not death: neither hath he pleasure in the destruction of the living.

14 For he created all things, that they might have their being: and the generations of the world were healthful; and there is no poison of destruction in them, nor the kingdom of death upon the earth:

15 (For righteousness is immortal:)

16 But ungodly men with their works and words called it to them: for when they thought to have it their friend, they consumed to nought, and made a covenant with it, because they are worthy to take part with it.

Chapter 2

1 For the ungodly said, reasoning with themselves, but not aright, Our life is short and tedious, and in the death of a man there is no remedy: neither was there any man known to have returned from the grave.

2 For we are born at all adventure: and we shall be hereafter as though we had never been: for the breath in our nostrils is as smoke, and a little spark in the moving of our heart:

3 Which being extinguished, our body shall be turned into ashes, and our spirit shall vanish as the soft air,

4 And our name shall be forgotten in time, and no man shall have our works in remembrance, and our life shall pass away as the trace of a cloud, and shall be dispersed as a mist, that is driven away with the beams of the sun, and overcome with the heat thereof.

5 For our time is a very shadow that passeth away; and after our end there is no returning: for it is fast sealed, so that no man cometh again.

6 Come on therefore, let us enjoy the good things that are present: and let us speedily use the creatures like as in youth.

7 Let us fill ourselves with costly wine and ointments: and let no flower of the spring pass by us:

8 Let us crown ourselves with rosebuds, before they be withered:

9 Let none of us go without his part of our voluptuousness: let us leave tokens of our joyfulness in every place: for this is our portion, and our lot is this.

10 Let us oppress the poor righteous man, let us not spare the widow, nor reverence the ancient gray hairs of the aged.

11 Let our strength be the law of justice: for that which is feeble is found to be nothing worth.

12 Therefore let us lie in wait for the righteous; because he is not for our turn, and he is clean contrary to our doings: he upbraideth us with our offending the law, and objecteth to our infamy the transgressions of our education.

13 He professeth to have the knowledge of God: and he calleth himself the child of the Lord.

14 He was made to reprove our thoughts.

15 He is grievous unto us even to behold: for his life is not like other men's, his ways are of another fashion.

16 We are esteemed of him as counterfeits: he abstaineth from our ways as from filthiness: he pronounceth the end of the just to be blessed, and maketh his boast that God is his father.

17 Let us see if his words be true: and let us prove what shall happen in the end of him.

18 For if the just man be the son of God, he will help him, and deliver him from the hand of his enemies.

19 Let us examine him with despitefulness and torture, that we may know his meekness, and prove his patience.

20 Let us condemn him with a shameful death: for by his own saying he shall be respected.

21 Such things they did imagine, and were deceived: for their own wickedness hath blinded them.

22 As for the mysteries of God, they kn ew them not: neither hoped they for the wages of righteousness, nor discerned a reward for blameless souls.

23 For God created man to be immortal, and made him to be an image of his own eternity.

24 Nevertheless through envy of the devil came death into the world: and they that do hold of his side do find it.

Chapter 3

1 But the souls of the righteous are in the hand of God, and there shall no torment touch them.

2 In the sight of the unwise they seemed to die: and their departure is taken for misery,

3 And their going from us to be utter destruction: but they are in peace.

4 For though they be punished in the sight of men, yet is their hope full of immortality.

5 And having been a little chastised, they shall be greatly rewarded: for God proved them, and found them worthy for himself.

6 As gold in the furnace hath he tried them, and received them as a burnt offering.

7 And in the time of their visitation they shall shine, and run to and fro like sparks among the stubble.

8 They shall judge the nations, and have dominion over the people, and their Lord shall reign for ever.

9 They that put their trust in him shall understand the truth: and such as be faithful in love shall abide with him: for grace and mercy is to his saints, and he hath care for his elect.

10 But the ungodly shall be punished according to their own imaginations, which have neglected the righteous, and forsaken the Lord.

11 For whoso despiseth wisdom and nurture, he is miserable, and their hope is vain, their labours unfruitful, and their works unprofitable:

12 Their wives are foolish, and their children wicked:

13 Their offspring is cursed. Wherefore blessed is the barren that is undefiled, which hath not known the sinful bed: she shall have fruit in the visitation of souls.

14 And blessed is the eunuch, which with his hands hath wrought no iniquity, nor imagined wicked things against God: for unto him shall be given the special gift of faith, and an inheritance in the temple of the Lord more acceptable to his mind.

15 For glorious is the fruit of good labours: and the root of wisdom shall never fall away.

16 As for the children of adulterers, they shall not come to their perfection, and the seed of an unrighteous bed shall be rooted out.

17 For though they live long, yet shall they be nothing regarded: and their last age shall be without honour.

18 Or, if they die quickly, they have no hope, neither comfort in the day of trial.

19 For horrible is the end of the unrighteous generation.

Chapter 4

1 Better it is to have no children, and to have virtue: for the memorial thereof is immortal: because it is known with God, and with men.

2 When it is present, men take example at it; and when it is gone, they desire it: it weareth a crown, and triumpheth for ever, having gotten the victory, striving for undefiled rewards.

3 But the multiplying brood of the ungodly shall not thrive, nor take deep rooting from bastard slips, nor lay any fast foundation.

4 For though they flourish in branches for a time; yet standing not last, they shall be shaken with the wind, and through the force of winds they shall be rooted out.

5 The imperfect branches shall be broken off, their fruit unprofitable, not ripe to eat, yea, meet for nothing.

6 For children begotten of unlawful beds are witnesses of wickedness against their parents in their trial.

7 But though the righteous be prevented with death, yet shall he be in rest.

8 For honourable age is not that which standeth in length of time, nor that is measured by number of years.

9 But wisdom is the gray hair unto men, and an unspotted life is old age.

10 He pleased God, and was beloved of him: so that living among sinners he was translated.

11 Yea speedily was he taken away, lest that wickedness should alter his understanding, or deceit beguile his soul.

12 For the bewitching of naughtiness doth obscure things that are honest; and the wandering of concupiscence doth undermine the simple mind.

13 He, being made perfect in a short time, fulfilled a long time:

14 For his soul pleased the Lord: therefore hasted he to take him away from among the wicked.

15 This the people saw, and understood it not, neither laid they up this in their minds, That his grace and mercy is with his saints, and that he hath respect unto his chosen.

16 Thus the righteous that is dead shall condemn the ungodly which are living; and youth that is soon perfected the many years and old age of the unrighteous.

17 For they shall see the end of the wise, and shall not understand what God in his counsel hath decreed of him, and to what end the Lord hath set him in safety.

18 They shall see him, and despise him; but God shall laugh them to scorn: and they shall hereafter be a vile carcase, and a reproach among the dead for evermore.

19 For he shall rend them, and cast them down headlong, that they shall be speechless; and he shall shake them from the foundation; and they shall be utterly laid waste, and be in sorrow; and their memorial shall perish.

20 And when they cast up the accounts of their sins, they shall come with fear: and their own iniquities shall convince them to their face.

Chapter 5

1 Then shall the righteous man stand in great boldness before the face of such as have afflicted him, and made no account of his labours.

2 When they see it, they shall be troubled with terrible fear, and shall be amazed at the strangeness of his salvation, so far beyond all that they looked for.

3 And they repenting and groaning for anguish of spirit shall say within themselves, This was he, whom we had sometimes in derision, and a proverb of reproach:

4 We fools accounted his life madness, and his end to be without honour:

5 How is he numbered among the children of God, and his lot is among the saints!

6 Therefore have we erred from the way of truth, and the light of righteousness hath not shined unto us, and the sun of righteousness rose not upon us.

7 We wearied ourselves in the way of wickedness and destruction: yea, we have gone through deserts, where there lay no way: but as for the way of the Lord, we have not known it.

8 What hath pride profited us? or what good hath riches with our vaunting brought us?

9 All those things are passed away like a shadow, and as a post that hasted by;

10 And as a ship that passeth over the waves of the water, which when it is gone by, the trace thereof cannot be found, neither the pathway of the keel in the waves;

11 Or as when a bird hath flown through the air, there is no token of her way to be found, but the light air being beaten with the stroke of her wings and parted with the violent noise and motion of them, is passed through, and therein afterwards no sign where she went is to be found;

12 Or like as when an arrow is shot at a mark, it parteth the air, which immediately cometh together again, so that a man cannot know where it went through:

13 Even so we in like manner, as soon as we were born, began to draw to our end, and had no sign of virtue to shew; but were consumed in our own wickedness.

14 For the hope of the Godly is like dust that is blown away with the wind; like a thin froth that is driven away with the storm; like as the smoke which is dispersed here and there with a tempest, and passeth away as the remembrance of a guest that tarrieth but a day.

15 But the righteous live for evermore; their reward also is with the Lord, and the care of them is with the most High.

16 Therefore shall they receive a glorious kingdom, and a beautiful crown from the Lord's hand: for with his right hand shall he cover them, and with his arm shall he protect them.

17 He shall take to him his jealousy for complete armour, and make the creature his weapon for the revenge of his enemies.

18 He shall put on righteousness as a breastplate, and true judgment instead of an helmet.

19 He shall take holiness for an invincible shield.

20 His severe wrath shall he sharpen for a sword, and the world shall fight with him against the unwise.

21 Then shall the right aiming thunderbolts go abroad; and from the clouds, as from a well drawn bow, shall they fly to the mark.

22 And hailstones full of wrath shall be cast as out of a stone bow, and the water of the sea shall rage against them, and the floods shall cruelly drown them.

23 Yea, a mighty wind shall stand up against them, and like a storm shall blow them away: thus iniquity shall lay waste the whole earth, and ill dealing shall overthrow the thrones of the mighty.

Chapter 6

1 Hear therefore, O ye kings, and understand; learn, ye that be judges of the ends of the earth.

2 Give ear, ye that rule the people, and glory in the multitude of nations.

3 For power is given you of the Lord, and sovereignty from the Highest, who shall try your works, and search out your counsels.

4 Because, being ministers of his kingdom, ye have not judged aright, nor kept the law, nor walked after the counsel of God;

5 Horribly and speedily shall he come upon you: for a sharp judgment shall be to them that be in high places.

6 For mercy will soon pardon the meanest: but mighty men shall be mightily tormented.

7 For he which is Lord over all shall fear no man's person, neither shall he stand in awe of any man's greatness: for he hath made the small and great, and careth for all alike.

8 But a sore trial shall come upon the mighty.

9 Unto you therefore, O kings, do I speak, that ye may learn wisdom, and not fall away.

10 For they that keep holiness holily shall be judged holy: and they that have learned such things shall find what to answer.

11 Wherefore set your affection upon my words; desire them, and ye shall be instructed.

12 Wisdom is glorious, and never fadeth away: yea, she is easily seen of them that love her, and found of such as seek her.

13 She preventeth them that desire her, in making herself first known unto them.

14 Whoso seeketh her early shall have no great travail: for he shall find her sitting at his doors.

15 To think therefore upon her is perfection of wisdom: and whoso watcheth for her shall quickly be without care.

16 For she goeth about seeking such as are worthy of her, sheweth herself favourably unto them in the ways, and meeteth them in every thought.

17 For the very true beginning of her is the desire of discipline; and the care of discipline is love;

18 And love is the keeping of her laws; and the giving heed unto her laws is the assurance of incorruption;

19 And incorruption maketh us near unto God:

20 Therefore the desire of wisdom bringeth to a kingdom.

21 If your delight be then in thrones and sceptres, O ye kings of the people, honour wisdom, that ye may reign for evermore.

22 As for wisdom, what she is, and how she came up, I will tell you, and will not hide mysteries from you: but will seek her out from the beginning of her nativity, and bring the knowledge of her into light, and will not pass over the truth.

23 Neither will I go with consuming envy; for such a man shall have no fellowship with wisdom.

24 But the multitude of the wise is the welfare of the world: and a wise king is the upholding of the people.

25 Receive therefore instruction through my words, and it shall do you good.

Chapter 7

1 I myself also am a mortal man, like to all, and the offspring of him that was first made of the earth,

2 And in my mother's womb was fashioned to be flesh in the time of ten months, being compacted in blood, of the seed of man, and the pleasure that came with sleep.

3 And when I was born, I drew in the common air, and fell upon the earth, which is of like nature, and the first voice which I uttered was crying, as all others do.

4 I was nursed in swaddling clothes, and that with cares.

5 For there is no king that had any other beginning of birth.

6 For all men have one entrance into life, and the like going out.

7 Wherefore I prayed, and understanding was given me: I called upon God, and the spirit of wisdom came to me.

8 I preferred her before sceptres and thrones, and esteemed riches nothing in comparison of her.

9 Neither compared I unto her any precious stone, because all gold in respect of her is as a little sand, and silver shall be counted as clay before her.

10 I loved her above health and beauty, and chose to have her instead of light: for the light that cometh from her never goeth out.

11 All good things together came to me with her, and innumerable riches in her hands.

12 And I rejoiced in them all, because wisdom goeth before them: and I knew not that she was the mother of them.

13 I learned diligently, and do communicate her liberally: I do not hide her riches.

14 For she is a treasure unto men that never faileth: which they that use become the friends of God, being commended for the gifts that come from learning.

15 God hath granted me to speak as I would, and to conceive as is meet for the things that are given me: because it is he that leadeth unto wisdom, and directeth the wise.

16 For in his hand are both we and our words; all wisdom also, and knowledge of workmanship.

17 For he hath given me certain knowledge of the things that are, namely, to know how the world was made, and the operation of the elements:

18 The beginning, ending, and midst of the times: the alterations of the turning of the sun, and the change of seasons:

19 The circuits of years, and the positions of stars:

20 The natures of living creatures, and the furies of wild beasts: the violence of winds, and the reasonings of men: the diversities of plants and the virtues of roots:

21 And all such things as are either secret or manifest, them I know.

22 For wisdom, which is the worker of all things, taught me: for in her is an understanding spirit holy, one only, manifold, subtil, lively, clear, undefiled, plain, not subject to hurt, loving the thing that is good quick, which cannot be letted, ready to do good,

23 Kind to man, steadfast, sure, free from care, having all power, overseeing all things, and going through all understanding, pure, and most subtil, spirits.

24 For wisdom is more moving than any motion: she passeth and goeth through all things by reason of her pureness.

25 For she is the breath of the power of God, and a pure influence flowing from the glory of the Almighty: therefore can no defiled thing fall into her.

26 For she is the brightness of the everlasting light, the unspotted mirror of the power of God, and the image of his goodness.

27 And being but one, she can do all things: and remaining in herself, she maketh all things new: and in all ages entering into holy souls, she maketh them friends of God, and prophets.

28 For God loveth none but him that dwelleth with wisdom.

29 For she is more beautiful than the sun, and above all the order of stars: being compared with the light, she is found before it.

30 For after this cometh night: but vice shall not prevail against wisdom.

Chapter 8

1 Wisdom reacheth from one end to another mightily: and sweetly doth she order all things.

2 I loved her, and sought her out from my youth, I desired to make her my spouse, and I was a lover of her beauty.

3 In that she is conversant with God, she magnifieth her nobility: yea, the Lord of all things himself loved her.

4 For she is privy to the mysteries of the knowledge of God, and a lover of his works.

5 If riches be a possession to be desired in this life; what is richer than wisdom, that worketh all things?

6 And if prudence work; who of all that are is a more cunning workman than she?

7 And if a man love righteousness her labours are virtues: for she teacheth temperance and prudence, justice and fortitude: which are such things, as en can have nothing more profitable in their life.

8 If a man desire much experience, she knoweth things of old, and conjectureth aright what is to come: she knoweth the subtilties of speeches, and can expound dark sentences: she foreseeth signs and wonders, and the events of seasons and times.

9 Therefore I purposed to take her to me to live with me, knowing that she would be a counsellor of good things, and a comfort in cares and grief.

10 For her sake I shall have estimation among the multitude, and honour with the elders, though I be young.

11 I shall be found of a quick conceit in judgment, and shall be admired in the sight of great men.

12 When I hold my tongue, they shall bide my leisure, and when I speak, they shall give good ear unto me: if I talk much, they shall lay their hands upon their mouth.

13 Moreover by the means of her I shall obtain immortality, and leave behind me an everlasting memorial to them that come after me.

14 I shall set the people in order, and the nations shall be subject unto me.

15 Horrible tyrants shall be afraid, when they do but hear of me; I shall be found good among the multitude, and valiant in war.

16 After I am come into mine house, I will repose myself with her: for her conversation hath no bitterness; and to live with her hath no sorrow, but mirth and joy.

17 Now when I considered these things in myself, and pondered them in my heart, how that to be allied unto wisdom is immortality;

18 And great pleasure it is to have her friendship; and in the works of her hands are infinite riches; and in the exercise of conference with her, prudence; and in talking with her, a good report; I went about seeking how to take her to me.

19 For I was a witty child, and had a good spirit.

20 Yea rather, being good, I came into a body undefiled.

21 Nevertheless, when I perceived that I could not otherwise obtain her, except God gave her me; and that was a point of wisdom also to know whose gift she was; I prayed unto the Lord, and besought him, and with my whole heart I said,

Chapter 9

1 O God of my fathers, and Lord of mercy, who hast made all things with thy word,

2 And ordained man through thy wisdom, that he should have dominion over the creatures which thou hast made,

3 And order the world according to equity and righteousness, and execute judgment with an upright heart:

4 Give me wisdom, that sitteth by thy throne; and reject me not from among thy children:

5 For I thy servant and son of thine handmaid am a feeble person, and of a short time, and too young for the understanding of judgment and laws.

6 For though a man be never so perfect among the children of men, yet if thy wisdom be not with him, he shall be nothing regarded.

7 Thou hast chosen me to be a king of thy people, and a judge of thy sons and daughters:

8 Thou hast commanded me to build a temple upon thy holy mount, and an altar in the city wherein thou dwellest, a resemblance of the holy tabernacle, which thou hast prepared from the beginning.

9 And wisdom was with thee: which knoweth thy works, and was present when thou madest the world, and knew what was acceptable in thy sight, and right in thy commandments.

10 O send her out of thy holy heavens, and from the throne of thy glory, that being present she may labour with me, that I may know what is pleasing unto thee.

11 For she knoweth and understandeth all things, and she shall lead me soberly in my doings, and preserve me in her power.

12 So shall my works be acceptable, and then shall I judge thy people righteously, and be worthy to sit in my father's seat.

13 For what man is he that can know the counsel of God? or who can think what the will of the Lord is?

14 For the thoughts of mortal men are miserable, and our devices are but uncertain.

15 For the corruptible body presseth down the soul, and the earthy tabernacle weigheth down the mind that museth upon many things.

16 And hardly do we guess aright at things that are upon earth, and with labour do we find the things that are before us: but the things that are in heaven who hath searched out?

17 And thy counsel who hath known, except thou give wisdom, and send thy Holy Spirit from above?

18 For so the ways of them which lived on the earth were reformed, and men were taught the things that are pleasing unto thee, and were saved through wisdom.

Chapter 10

1 She preserved the first formed father of the world, that was created alone, and brought him out of his fall,

2 And gave him power to rule all things.

3 But when the unrighteous went away from her in his anger, he perished also in the fury wherewith he murdered his brother.

4 For whose cause the earth being drowned with the flood, wisdom again preserved it, and directed the course of the righteous in a piece of wood of small value.

5 Moreover, the nations in their wicked conspiracy being confounded, she found out the righteous, and preserved him blameless unto God, and kept him strong against his tender compassion toward his son.

6 When the ungodly perished, she delivered the righteous man, who fled from the fire which fell down upon the five cities.

7 Of whose wickedness even to this day the waste land that smoketh is a testimony, and plants bearing fruit that never come to ripeness: and a standing pillar of salt is a monument of an unbelieving soul.

8 For regarding not wisdom, they gat not only this hurt, that they knew not the things which were good; but also left behind them to the world a memorial of their foolishness: so that in the things wherein they offended they could not so much as be hid.

9 Rut wisdom delivered from pain those that attended upon her.

10 When the righteous fled from his brother's wrath she guided him in right paths, shewed him the kingdom of God, and gave him knowledge of holy things, made him rich in his travels, and multiplied the fruit of his labours.

11 In the covetousness of such as oppressed him she stood by him, and made him rich.

12 She defended him from his enemies, and kept him safe from those that lay in wait, and in a sore conflict she gave him the victory; that he might know that goodness is stronger than all.

13 When the righteous was sold, she forsook him not, but delivered him from sin: she went down with him into the pit,

14 And left him not in bonds, till she brought him the sceptre of the kingdom, and power against those that oppressed him: as for them that had accused him, she shewed them to be liars, and gave him perpetual glory.

15 She delivered the righteous people and blameless seed from the nation that oppressed them.

16 She entered into the soul of the servant of the Lord, and withstood dreadful kings in wonders and signs;

17 Rendered to the righteous a reward of their labours, guided them in a marvellous way, and was unto them for a cover by day, and a light of stars in the night season;

18 Brought them through the Red sea, and led them through much water:

19 But she drowned their enemies, and cast them up out of the bottom of the deep.

20 Therefore the righteous spoiled the ungodly, and praised thy holy name, O Lord, and magnified with one accord thine hand, that fought for them.

21 For wisdom opened the mouth of the dumb, and made the tongues of them that cannot speak eloquent.

Chapter 11

1 She prospered their works in the hand of the holy prophet.

2 They went through the wilderness that was not inhabited, and pitched tents in places where there lay no way.

3 They stood against their enemies, and were avenged of their adversaries.

4 When they were thirsty, they called upon thee, and water was given them out of the flinty rock, and their thirst was quenched out of the hard stone.

5 For by what things their enemies were punished, by the same they in their need were benefited.

6 For instead of of a perpetual running river troubled with foul blood,

7 For a manifest reproof of that commandment, whereby the infants were slain, thou gavest unto them abundance of water by a means which they hoped not for:

8 Declaring by that thirst then how thou hadst punished their adversaries.

9 For when they were tried albeit but in mercy chastised, they knew how the ungodly were judged in wrath and tormented, thirsting in another manner than the just.

10 For these thou didst admonish and try, as a father: but the other, as a severe king, thou didst condemn and punish.

11 Whether they were absent or present, they were vexed alike.

12 For a double grief came upon them, and a groaning for the remembrance of things past.

13 For when they heard by their own punishments the other to be benefited, they had some feeling of the Lord.

14 For whom they respected with scorn, when he was long before thrown out at the casting forth of the infants, him in the end, when they saw what came to pass, they admired.

15 But for the foolish devices of their wickedness, wherewith being deceived they worshipped serpents void of reason, and vile beasts, thou didst send a multitude of unreasonable beasts upon them for vengeance;

16 That they might know, that wherewithal a man sinneth, by the same also shall he be punished.

17 For thy Almighty hand, that made the world of matter without form, wanted not means to send among them a multitude of bears or fierce lions,

18 Or unknown wild beasts, full of rage, newly created, breathing out either a fiery vapour, or filthy scents of scattered smoke, or shooting horrible sparkles out of their eyes:

19 Whereof not only the harm might dispatch them at once, but also the terrible sight utterly destroy them.

20 Yea, and without these might they have fallen down with one blast, being persecuted of vengeance, and scattered abroad through the breath of thy power: but thou hast ordered all things in measure and number and weight.

21 For thou canst shew thy great strength at all times when thou wilt; and who may withstand the power of thine arm?

22 For the whole world before thee is as a little grain of the balance, yea, as a drop of the morning dew that falleth down upon the earth.

23 But thou hast mercy upon all; for thou canst do all things, and winkest at the sins of men, because they should amend.

24 For thou lovest all the things that are, and abhorrest nothing which thou hast made: for never wouldest thou have made any thing, if thou hadst hated it.

25 And how could any thing have endured, if it had not been thy will? or been preserved, if not called by thee?

26 But thou sparest all: for they are thine, O Lord, thou lover of souls.

Chapter 12

1 For thine incorruptible Spirit is in all things.

2 Therefore chastenest thou them by little and little that offend, and warnest them by putting them in remembrance wherein they have offended, that leaving their wickedness they may believe on thee, O Lord.

3 For it was thy will to destroy by the hands of our fathers both those old inhabitants of thy holy land,

4 Whom thou hatedst for doing most odious works of witchcrafts, and wicked sacrifices;

5 And also those merciless murderers of children, and devourers of man's flesh, and the feasts of blood,

6 With their priests out of the midst of their idolatrous crew, and the parents, that killed with their own hands souls destitute of help:

7 That the land, which thou esteemedst above all other, might receive a worthy colony of God's children.

8 Nevertheless even those thou sparedst as men, and didst send wasps, forerunners of thine host, to destroy them by little and little.

9 Not that thou wast unable to bring the ungodly under the hand of the righteous in battle, or to destroy them at once with cruel beasts, or with one rough word:

10 But executing thy judgments upon them by little and little, thou gavest them place of repentance, not being ignorant that they were a naughty generation, and that their malice was bred in them, and that their cogitation would never be changed.

11 For it was a cursed seed from the beginning; neither didst thou for fear of any man give them pardon for those things wherein they sinned.

12 For who shall say, What hast thou done? or who shall withstand thy judgment? or who shall accuse thee for the nations that perish, whom thou made? or who shall come to stand against thee, to be revenged for the unrighteous men?

13 For neither is there any God but thou that careth for all, to whom thou mightest shew that thy judgment is not unright.

14 Neither shall king or tyrant be able to set his face against thee for any whom thou hast punished.

15 Forsomuch then as thou art righteous thyself, thou orderest all things righteously: thinking it not agreeable with thy power to condemn him that hath not deserved to be punished.

16 For thy power is the beginning of righteousness, and because thou art the Lord of all, it maketh thee to be gracious unto all.

17 For when men will not believe that thou art of a full power, thou shewest thy strength, and among them that know it thou makest their boldness manifest.

18 But thou, mastering thy power, judgest with equity, and orderest us with great favour: for thou mayest use power when thou wilt.

19 But by such works hast thou taught thy people that the just man should be merciful, and hast made thy children to be of a good hope that thou givest repentance for sins.

20 For if thou didst punish the enemies of thy children, and the condemned to death, with such deliberation, giving them time and place, whereby they might be delivered from their malice:

21 With how great circumspection didst thou judge thine own sons, unto whose fathers thou hast sworn, and made covenants of good promises?

22 Therefore, whereas thou dost chasten us, thou scourgest our enemies a thousand times more, to the intent that, when we judge, we should carefully think of thy goodness, and when we ourselves are judged, we should look for mercy.

23 Wherefore, whereas men have lived dissolutely and unrighteously, thou hast tormented them with their own abominations.

24 For they went astray very far in the ways of error, and held them for gods, which even among the beasts of their enemies were despised, being deceived, as children of no understanding.

25 Therefore unto them, as to children without the use of reason, thou didst send a judgment to mock them.

26 But they that would not be reformed by that correction, wherein he dallied with them, shall feel a judgment worthy of God.

27 For, look, for what things they grudged, when they were punished, that is, for them whom they thought to be gods; [now] being punished in them, when they saw it, they acknowledged him to be the true God, whom before they denied to know: and therefore came extreme damnation upon them.

Chapter 13

1 Surely vain are all men by nature, who are ignorant of God, and could not out of the good things that are seen know him that is: neither by considering the works did they acknowledge the workmaster;

2 But deemed either fire, or wind, or the swift air, or the circle of the stars, or the violent water, or the lights of heaven, to be the gods which govern the world.

3 With whose beauty if they being delighted took them to be gods; let them know how much better the Lord of them is: for the first author of beauty hath created them.

4 But if they were astonished at their power and virtue, let them understand by them, how much mightier he is that made them.

5 For by the greatness and beauty of the creatures proportionably the maker of them is seen.

6 But yet for this they are the less to be blamed: for they peradventure err, seeking God, and desirous to find him.

7 For being conversant in his works they search him diligently, and believe their sight: because the things are beautiful that are seen.

8 Howbeit neither are they to be pardoned.

9 For if they were able to know so much, that they could aim at the world; how did they not sooner find out the Lord thereof?

10 But miserable are they, and in dead things is their hope, who call them gods, which are the works of men's hands, gold and silver, to shew art in, and resemblances of beasts, or a stone good for nothing, the work of an ancient hand.

11 Now a carpenter that felleth timber, after he hath sawn down a tree meet for the purpose, and taken off all the bark skilfully round about, and hath wrought it handsomely, and made a vessel thereof fit for the service of man's life;

12 And after spending the refuse of his work to dress his meat, hath filled himself;

13 And taking the very refuse among those which served to no use, being a crooked piece of wood, and full of knots, hath carved it diligently, when he had nothing else to do, and formed it by the skill of his understanding, and fashioned it to the image of a man;

14 Or made it like some vile beast, laying it over with vermilion, and with paint colouring it red, and covering every spot therein;

15 And when he had made a convenient room for it, set it in a wall, and made it fast with iron:

16 For he provided for it that it might not fall, knowing that it was unable to help itself; for it is an image, and hath need of help:

17 Then maketh he prayer for his goods, for his wife and children, and is not ashamed to speak to that which hath no life.

18 For health he calleth upon that which is weak: for life prayeth to that which is dead; for aid humbly beseecheth that which hath least means to help: and for a good journey he asketh of that which cannot set a foot forward:

19 And for gaining and getting, and for good success of his hands, asketh ability to do of him, that is most unable to do any thing.

Chapter 14

1 Again, one preparing himself to sail, and about to pass through the raging waves, calleth upon a piece of wood more rotten than the vessel that carrieth him.

2 For verily desire of gain devised that, and the workman built it by his skill.

3 But thy providence, O Father, governeth it: for thou hast made a way in the sea, and a safe path in the waves;

4 Shewing that thou canst save from all danger: yea, though a man went to sea without art.

5 Nevertheless thou wouldest not that the works of thy wisdom should be idle, and therefore do men commit their lives to a small piece of wood, and passing the rough sea in a weak vessel are saved.

6 For in the old time also, when the proud giants perished, the hope of the world governed by thy hand escaped in a weak vessel, and left to all ages a seed of generation.

7 For blessed is the wood whereby righteousness cometh.

8 But that which is made with hands is cursed, as well it, as he that made it: he, because he made it; and it, because, being corruptible, it was called god.

9 For the ungodly and his ungodliness are both alike hateful unto God.

10 For that which is made shall be punished together with him that made it.

11 Therefore even upon the idols of the Gentiles shall there be a visitation: because in the creature of God they are become an abomination, and stumblingblocks to the souls of men, and a snare to the feet of the unwise.

12 For the devising of idols was the beginning of spiritual fornication, and the invention of them the corruption of life.

13 For neither were they from the beginning, neither shall they be for ever.

14 For by the vain glory of men they entered into the world, and therefore shall they come shortly to an end.

15 For a father afflicted with untimely mourning, when he hath made an image of his child soon taken away, now honoured him as a god, which was then a dead man, and delivered to those that were under him ceremonies and sacrifices.

16 Thus in process of time an ungodly custom grown strong was kept as a law, and graven images were worshipped by the commandments of kings.

17 Whom men could not honour in presence, because they dwelt far off, they took the counterfeit of his visage from far, and made an express image of a king whom they honoured, to the end that by this their forwardness they might flatter him that was absent, as if he were present.

18 Also the singular diligence of the artificer did help to set forward the ignorant to more superstition.

19 For he, peradventure willing to please one in authority, forced all his skill to make the resemblance of the best fashion.

20 And so the multitude, allured by the grace of the work, took him now for a god, which a little before was but honoured.

21 And this was an occasion to deceive the world: for men, serving either calamity or tyranny, did ascribe unto stones and stocks the incommunicable name.

22 Moreover this was not enough for them, that they erred in the knowledge of God; but whereas they lived in the great war of ignorance, those so great plagues called they peace.

23 For whilst they slew their children in sacrifices, or used secret ceremonies, or made revellings of strange rites;

24 They kept neither lives nor marriages any longer undefiled: but either one slew another traiterously, or grieved him by adultery.

25 So that there reigned in all men without exception blood, manslaughter, theft, and dissimulation, corruption, unfaithfulness, tumults, perjury,

26 Disquieting of good men, forgetfulness of good turns, defiling of souls, changing of kind, disorder in marriages, adultery, and shameless uncleanness.

27 For the worshipping of idols not to be named is the beginning, the cause, and the end, of all evil.

28 For either they are mad when they be merry, or prophesy lies, or live unjustly, or else lightly forswear themselves.

29 For insomuch as their trust is in idols, which have no life; though they swear falsely, yet they look not to be hurt.

30 Howbeit for both causes shall they be justly punished: both because they thought not well of God, giving heed unto idols, and also unjustly swore in deceit, despising holiness.

31 For it is not the power of them by whom they swear: but it is the just vengeance of sinners, that punisheth always the offence of the ungodly.

Chapter 15

1 But thou, O God, art gracious and true, longsuffering, and in mercy ordering all things,

2 For if we sin, we are thine, knowing thy power: but we will not sin, knowing that we are counted thine.

3 For to know thee is perfect righteousness: yea, to know thy power is the root of immortality.

4 For neither did the mischievous invention of men deceive us, nor an image spotted with divers colours, the painter's fruitless labour;

5 The sight whereof enticeth fools to lust after it, and so they desire the form of a dead image, that hath no breath.

6 Both they that make them, they that desire them, and they that worship them, are lovers of evil things, and are worthy to have such things to trust upon.

7 For the potter, tempering soft earth, fashioneth every vessel with much labour for our service: yea, of the same clay he maketh both the vessels that serve for clean uses, and likewise also all such as serve to the contrary: but what is the use of either sort, the potter himself is the judge.

8 And employing his labours lewdly, he maketh a vain god of the same clay, even he which a little before was made of earth himself, and within a little while after returneth to the same, out when his life which was lent him shall be demanded.

9 Notwithstanding his care is, not that he shall have much labour, nor that his life is short: but striveth to excel goldsmiths and silversmiths, and endeavoureth to do like the workers in brass, and counteth it his glory to make counterfeit things.

10 His heart is ashes, his hope is more vile than earth, and his life of less value than clay:

11 Forasmuch as he knew not his Maker, and him that inspired into him an active soul, and breathed in a living spirit.

12 But they counted our life a pastime, and our time here a market for gain: for, say they, we must be getting every way, though it be by evil means.

13 For this man, that of earthly matter maketh brittle vessels and graven images, knoweth himself to offend above all others.

14 And all the enemies of thy people, that hold them in subjection, are most foolish, and are more miserable than very babes.

15 For they counted all the idols of the heathen to be gods: which neither have the use of eyes to see, nor noses to draw breath, nor ears to hear, nor fingers of hands to handle; and as for their feet, they are slow to go.

16 For man made them, and he that borrowed his own spirit fashioned them: but no man can make a god like unto himself.

17 For being mortal, he worketh a dead thing with wicked hands: for he himself is better than the things which he worshippeth: whereas he lived once, but they never.

18 Yea, they worshipped those beasts also that are most hateful: for being compared together, some are worse than others.

19 Neither are they beautiful, so much as to be desired in respect of beasts: but they went without the praise of God and his blessing.

Chapter 16

1 Therefore by the like were they punished worthily, and by the multitude of beasts tormented.

2 Instead of which punishment, dealing graciously with thine own people, thou preparedst for them meat of a strange taste, even quails to stir up their appetite:

3 To the end that they, desiring food, might for the ugly sight of the beasts sent among them lothe even that, which they must needs desire; but these, suffering penury for a short space, might be made partakers of a strange taste.

4 For it was requisite, that upon them exercising tyranny should come penury, which they could not avoid: but to these it should only be shewed how their enemies were tormented.

5 For when the horrible fierceness of beasts came upon these, and they perished with the stings of crooked serpents, thy wrath endured not for ever:

6 But they were troubled for a small season, that they might be admonished, having a sign of salvation, to put them in remembrance of the commandment of thy law.

7 For he that turned himself toward it was not saved by the thing that he saw, but by thee, that art the Saviour of all.

8 And in this thou madest thine enemies confess, that it is thou who deliverest from all evil:

9 For them the bitings of grasshoppers and flies killed, neither was there found any remedy for their life: for they were worthy to be punished by such.

10 But thy sons not the very teeth of venomous dragons overcame: for thy mercy was ever by them, and healed them.

11 For they were pricked, that they should remember thy words; and were quickly saved, that not falling into deep forgetfulness, they might be continually mindful of thy goodness.

12 For it was neither herb, nor mollifying plaister, that restored them to health: but thy word, O Lord, which healeth all things.

13 For thou hast power of life and death: thou leadest to the gates of hell, and bringest up again.

14 A man indeed killeth through his malice: and the spirit, when it is gone forth, returneth not; neither the soul received up cometh again.

15 But it is not possible to escape thine hand.

16 For the ungodly, that denied to know thee, were scourged by the strength of thine arm: with strange rains, hails, and showers, were they persecuted, that they could not avoid, and through fire were they consumed.

17 For, which is most to be wondered at, the fire had more force in the water, that quencheth all things: for the world fighteth for the righteous.

18 For sometime the flame was mitigated, that it might not burn up the beasts that were sent against the ungodly; but themselves might see and perceive that they were persecuted with the judgment of God.

19 And at another time it burneth even in the midst of water above the power of fire, that it might destroy the fruits of an unjust land.

20 Instead whereof thou feddest thine own people with angels' food, and didst send them from heaven bread prepared without their labour, able to content every man's delight, and agreeing to every taste.

21 For thy sustenance declared thy sweetness unto thy children, and serving to the appetite of the eater, tempered itself to every man's liking.

22 But snow and ice endured the fire, and melted not, that they might know that fire burning in the hail, and sparkling in the rain, did destroy the fruits of the enemies.

23 But this again did even forget his own strength, that the righteous might be nourished.

24 For the creature that serveth thee, who art the Maker increaseth his strength against the unrighteous for their punishment, and abateth his strength for the benefit of such as put their trust in thee.

25 Therefore even then was it altered into all fashions, and was obedient to thy grace, that nourisheth all things, according to the desire of them that had need:

26 That thy children, O Lord, whom thou lovest, might know, that it is not the growing of fruits that nourisheth man: but that it is thy word, which preserveth them that put their trust in thee.

27 For that which was not destroyed of the fire, being warmed with a little sunbeam, soon melted away:

28 That it might be known, that we must prevent the sun to give thee thanks, and at the dayspring pray unto thee.

29 For the hope of the unthankful shall melt away as the winter's hoar frost, and shall run away as unprofitable water.

Chapter 17

1 For great are thy judgments, and cannot be expressed: therefore unnurtured souls have erred.

2 For when unrighteous men thought to oppress the holy nation; they being shut up in their houses, the prisoners of darkness, and fettered with the bonds of a long night, lay [there] exiled from the eternal providence.

3 For while they supposed to lie hid in their secret sins, they were scattered under a dark veil of forgetfulness, being horribly astonished, and troubled with [strange] apparitions.

4 For neither might the corner that held them keep them from fear: but noises [as of waters] falling down sounded about them, and sad visions appeared unto them with heavy countenances.

5 No power of the fire might give them light: neither could the bright flames of the stars endure to lighten that horrible night.

6 Only there appeared unto them a fire kindled of itself, very dreadful: for being much terrified, they thought the things which they saw to be worse than the sight they saw not.

7 As for the illusions of art magick, they were put down, and their vaunting in wisdom was reproved with disgrace.

8 For they, that promised to drive away terrors and troubles from a sick soul, were sick themselves of fear, worthy to be laughed at.

9 For though no terrible thing did fear them; yet being scared with beasts that passed by, and hissing of serpents,

10 They died for fear, denying that they saw the air, which could of no side be avoided.

11 For wickedness, condemned by her own witness, is very timorous, and being pressed with conscience, always forecasteth grievous things.

12 For fear is nothing else but a betraying of the succours which reason offereth.

13 And the expectation from within, being less, counteth the ignorance more than the cause which bringeth the torment.

14 But they sleeping the same sleep that night, which was indeed intolerable, and which came upon them out of the bottoms of inevitable hell,

15 Were partly vexed with monstrous apparitions, and partly fainted, their heart failing them: for a sudden fear, and not looked for, came upon them.

16 So then whosoever there fell down was straitly kept, shut up in a prison without iron bars,

17 For whether he were husbandman, or shepherd, or a labourer in the field, he was overtaken, and endured that necessity, which could not be avoided: for they were all bound with one chain of darkness.

18 Whether it were a whistling wind, or a melodious noise of birds among the spreading branches, or a pleasing fall of water running violently,

19 Or a terrible sound of stones cast down, or a running that could not be seen of skipping beasts, or a roaring voice of most savage wild beasts, or a rebounding echo from the hollow mountains; these things made them to swoon for fear.

20 For the whole world shined with clear light, and none were hindered in their labour:

21 Over them only was spread an heavy night, an image of that darkness which should afterward receive them: but yet were they unto themselves more grievous than the darkness.

Chapter 18

1 Nevertheless thy saints had a very great light, whose voice they hearing, and not seeing their shape, because they also had not suffered the same things, they counted them happy.

2 But for that they did not hurt them now, of whom they had been wronged before, they thanked them, and besought them pardon for that they had been enemies.

3 Instead whereof thou gavest them a burning pillar of fire, both to be a guide of the unknown journey, and an harmless sun to entertain them honourably.

4 For they were worthy to be deprived of light and imprisoned in darkness, who had kept thy sons shut up, by whom the uncorrupt light of the law was to be given unto the world.

5 And when they had determined to slay the babes of the saints, one child being cast forth, and saved, to reprove them, thou tookest away the multitude of their children, and destroyedst them altogether in a mighty water.

6 Of that night were our fathers certified afore, that assuredly knowing unto what oaths they had given credence, they might afterwards be of good cheer.

7 So of thy people was accepted both the salvation of the righteous, and destruction of the enemies.

8 For wherewith thou didst punish our adversaries, by the same thou didst glorify us, whom thou hadst called.

9 For the righteous children of good men did sacrifice secretly, and with one consent made a holy law, that the saints should be like partakers of the same good and evil, the fathers now singing out the songs of praise.

10 But on the other side there sounded an ill according cry of the enemies, and a lamentable noise was carried abroad for children that were bewailed.

11 The master and the servant were punished after one manner; and like as the king, so suffered the common person.

12 So they all together had innumerable dead with one kind of death; neither were the living sufficient to bury them: for in one moment the noblest offspring of them was destroyed.

13 For whereas they would not believe any thing by reason of the enchantments; upon the destruction of the firstborn, they acknowledged this people to be the sons of God.

14 For while all things were in quiet silence, and that night was in the midst of her swift course,

15 Thine Almighty word leaped down from heaven out of thy royal throne, as a fierce man of war into the midst of a land of destruction,

16 And brought thine unfeigned commandment as a sharp sword, and standing up filled all things with death; and it touched the heaven, but it stood upon the earth.

17 Then suddenly visions of horrible dreams troubled them sore, and terrors came upon them unlooked for.

18 And one thrown here, and another there, half dead, shewed the cause of his death.

19 For the dreams that troubled them did foreshew this, lest they should perish, and not know why they were afflicted.

20 Yea, the tasting of death touched the righteous also, and there was a destruction of the multitude in the wilderness: but the wrath endured not long.

21 For then the blameless man made haste, and stood forth to defend them; and bringing the shield of his proper ministry, even prayer, and the propitiation of incense, set himself against the wrath, and so brought the calamity to an end, declaring that he was thy servant.

22 So he overcame the destroyer, not with strength of body, nor force of arms, but with a word subdued him that punished, alleging the oaths and covenants made with the fathers.

23 For when the dead were now fallen down by heaps one upon another, standing between, he stayed the wrath, and parted the way to the living.

24 For in the long garment was the whole world, and in the four rows of the stones was the glory of the fathers graven, and thy Majesty upon the daidem of his head.

25 Unto these the destroyer gave place, and was afraid of them: for it was enough that they only tasted of the wrath.

Chapter 19

1 As for the ungodly, wrath came upon them without mercy unto the end: for he knew before what they would do;

2 How that having given them leave to depart, and sent them hastily away, they would repent and pursue them.

3 For whilst they were yet mourning and making lamentation at the graves of the dead, they added another foolish device, and pursued them as fugitives, whom they had intreated to be gone.

4 For the destiny, whereof they were worthy, drew them unto this end, and made them forget the things that had already happened, that they might fulfil the punishment which was wanting to their torments:

5 And that thy people might pass a wonderful way: but they might find a strange death.

6 For the whole creature in his proper kind was fashioned again anew, serving the peculiar commandments that were given unto them, that thy children might be kept without hurt:

7 As namely, a cloud shadowing the camp; and where water stood before, dry land appeared; and out of the Red sea a way without impediment; and out of the violent stream a green field:

8 Wherethrough all the people went that were defended with thy hand, seeing thy marvellous strange wonders.

9 For they went at large like horses, and leaped like lambs, praising thee, O Lord, who hadst delivered them.

10 For they were yet mindful of the things that were done while they sojourned in the strange land, how the ground brought forth flies instead of cattle, and how the river cast up a multitude of frogs instead of fishes.

11 But afterwards they saw a new generation of fowls, when, being led with their appetite, they asked delicate meats.

12 For quails came up unto them from the sea for their contentment.

13 And punishments came upon the sinners not without former signs by the force of thunders: for they suffered justly according to their own wickedness, insomuch as they used a more hard and hateful behaviour toward strangers.

14 For the Sodomites did not receive those, whom they knew not when they came: but these brought friends into bondage, that had well deserved of them.

15 And not only so, but peradventure some respect shall be had of those, because they used strangers not friendly:

16 But these very grievously afflicted them, whom they had received with feastings, and were already made partakers of the same laws with them.

17 Therefore even with blindness were these stricken, as those were at the doors of the righteous man: when, being compassed about with horrible great darkness, every one sought the passage of his own doors.

18 For the elements were changed in themselves by a kind of harmony, like as in a psaltery notes change the name of the tune, and yet are always sounds; which may well be perceived by the sight of the things that have been done.

19 For earthly things were turned into watery, and the things, that before swam in the water, now went upon the ground.

20 The fire had power in the water, forgetting his own virtue: and the water forgat his own quenching nature.

21 On the other side, the flames wasted not the flesh of the corruptible living things, though they walked therein; neither melted they the icy kind of heavenly meat that was of nature apt to melt.

22 For in all things, O Lord, thou didst magnify thy people, and glorify them, neither didst thou lightly regard them: but didst assist them in every time and place.

The Song of Solomon (The Song of Songs)

(King James Version)

Chapter 1

1 The song of songs, which is Solomon's.

2 Let him kiss me with the kisses of his mouth: for thy love is better than wine.

3 Because of the savour of thy good ointments thy name is as ointment poured forth, therefore do the virgins love thee.

4 Draw me, we will run after thee: the king hath brought me into his chambers: we will be glad and rejoice in thee, we will remember thy love more than wine: the upright love thee.

5 I am black, but comely, O ye daughters of Jerusalem, as the tents of Kedar, as the curtains of Solomon.

6 Look not upon me, because I am black, because the sun hath looked upon me: my mother's children were angry with me; they made me the keeper of the vineyards; but mine own vineyard have I not kept.

7 Tell me, O thou whom my soul loveth, where thou feedest, where thou makest thy flock to rest at noon: for why should I be as one that turneth aside by the flocks of thy companions?

8 If thou know not, O thou fairest among women, go thy way forth by the footsteps of the flock, and feed thy kids beside the shepherds' tents.

9 I have compared thee, O my love, to a company of horses in Pharaoh's chariots.

10 Thy cheeks are comely with rows of jewels, thy neck with chains of gold.

11 We will make thee borders of gold with studs of silver.

12 While the king sitteth at his table, my spikenard sendeth forth the smell thereof.

13 A bundle of myrrh is my well-beloved unto me; he shall lie all night betwixt my breasts.

14 My beloved is unto me as a cluster of camphire in the vineyards of Engedi.

15 Behold, thou art fair, my love; behold, thou art fair; thou hast doves' eyes.

16 Behold, thou art fair, my beloved, yea, pleasant: also our bed is green.

17 The beams of our house are cedar, and our rafters of fir.

Chapter 2

1 I am the rose of Sharon, and the lily of the valleys.

2 As the lily among thorns, so is my love among the daughters.

3 As the apple tree among the trees of the wood, so is my beloved among the sons. I sat down under his shadow with great delight, and his fruit was sweet to my taste.

4 He brought me to the banqueting house, and his banner over me was love.

5 Stay me with flagons, comfort me with apples: for I am sick of love.

6 His left hand is under my head, and his right hand doth embrace me.

7 I charge you, O ye daughters of Jerusalem, by the roes, and by the hinds of the field, that ye stir not up, nor awake my love, till he please.

8 The voice of my beloved! behold, he cometh leaping upon the mountains, skipping upon the hills.

9 My beloved is like a roe or a young hart: behold, he standeth behind our wall, he looketh forth at the windows, shewing himself through the lattice.

10 My beloved spake, and said unto me, Rise up, my love, my fair one, and come away.

11 For, lo, the winter is past, the rain is over and gone;

12 The flowers appear on the earth; the time of the singing of birds is come, and the voice of the turtle is heard in our land;

13 The fig tree putteth forth her green figs, and the vines with the tender grape give a good smell. Arise, my love, my fair one, and come away.

14 O my dove, that art in the clefts of the rock, in the secret places of the stairs, let me see thy countenance, let me hear thy voice; for sweet is thy voice, and thy countenance is comely.

15 Take us the foxes, the little foxes, that spoil the vines: for our vines have tender grapes.

16 My beloved is mine, and I am his: he feedeth among the lilies.

17 Until the day break, and the shadows flee away, turn, my beloved, and be thou like a roe or a young hart upon the mountains of Bether.

Chapter 3

1 By night on my bed I sought him whom my soul loveth: I sought him, but I found him not.

2 I will rise now, and go about the city in the streets, and in the broad ways I will seek him whom my soul loveth: I sought him, but I found him not.

3 The watchmen that go about the city found me: to whom I said, Saw ye him whom my soul loveth?

4 It was but a little that I passed from them, but I found him whom my soul loveth: I held him, and would not let him go, until I had brought him into my mother's house, and into the chamber of her that conceived me.

5 I charge you, O ye daughters of Jerusalem, by the roes, and by the hinds of the field, that ye stir not up, nor awake my love, till he please.

6 Who is this that cometh out of the wilderness like pillars of smoke, perfumed with myrrh and frankincense, with all powders of the merchant?

7 Behold his bed, which is Solomon's; threescore valiant men are about it, of the valiant of Israel.

8 They all hold swords, being expert in war: every man hath his sword upon his thigh because of fear in the night.

9 King Solomon made himself a chariot of the wood of Lebanon.

10 He made the pillars thereof of silver, the bottom thereof of gold, the covering of it of purple, the midst thereof being paved with love, for the daughters of Jerusalem.

11 Go forth, O ye daughters of Zion, and behold king Solomon with the crown wherewith his mother crowned him in the day of his espousals, and in the day of the gladness of his heart.

Chapter 4

1 Behold, thou art fair, my love; behold, thou art fair; thou hast doves' eyes within thy locks: thy hair is as a flock of goats, that appear from mount Gilead.

2 Thy teeth are like a flock of sheep that are even shorn, which came up from the washing; whereof every one bear twins, and none is barren among them.

3 Thy lips are like a thread of scarlet, and thy speech is comely: thy temples are like a piece of a pomegranate within thy locks.

4 Thy neck is like the tower of David builded for an armoury, whereon there hang a thousand bucklers, all shields of mighty men.

5 Thy two breasts are like two young roes that are twins, which feed among the lilies.

6 Until the day break, and the shadows flee away, I will get me to the mountain of myrrh, and to the hill of frankincense.

7 Thou art all fair, my love; there is no spot in thee.

8 Come with me from Lebanon, my spouse, with me from Lebanon: look from the top of Amana, from the top of Shenir and Hermon, from the lions' dens, from the mountains of the leopards.

9 Thou hast ravished my heart, my sister, my spouse; thou hast ravished my heart with one of thine eyes, with one chain of thy neck.

10 How fair is thy love, my sister, my spouse! how much better is thy love than wine! and the smell of thine ointments than all spices!

11 Thy lips, O my spouse, drop as the honeycomb: honey and milk are under thy tongue; and the smell of thy garments is like the smell of Lebanon.

12 A garden inclosed is my sister, my spouse; a spring shut up, a fountain sealed.

13 Thy plants are an orchard of pomegranates, with pleasant fruits; camphire, with spikenard, 14 Spikenard and saffron; calamus and cinnamon, with all trees of frankincense; myrrh and aloes, with all the chief spices:

15 A fountain of gardens, a well of living waters, and streams from Lebanon.

16 Awake, O north wind; and come, thou south; blow upon my garden, that the spices thereof may flow out. Let my beloved come into his garden, and eat his pleasant fruits.

Chapter 5

1 I am come into my garden, my sister, my spouse: I have gathered my myrrh with my spice; I have eaten my honeycomb with my honey; I have drunk my wine with my milk: eat, O friends; drink, yea, drink abundantly, O beloved.

2 I sleep, but my heart waketh: it is the voice of my beloved that knocketh, saying, Open to me, my sister, my love, my dove, my undefiled: for my head is filled with dew, and my locks with the drops of the night.

3 I have put off my coat; how shall I put it on? I have washed my feet; how shall I defile them?

4 My beloved put in his hand by the hole of the door, and my bowels were moved for him.

5 I rose up to open to my beloved; and my hands dropped with myrrh, and my fingers with sweet smelling myrrh, upon the handles of the lock.

6 I opened to my beloved; but my beloved had withdrawn himself, and was gone: my soul failed when he spake: I sought him, but I could not find him; I called him, but he gave me no answer.

7 The watchmen that went about the city found me, they smote me, they wounded me; the keepers of the walls took away my veil from me.

8 I charge you, O daughters of Jerusalem, if ye find my beloved, that ye tell him, that I am sick of love.

9 What is thy beloved more than another beloved, O thou fairest among women? what is thy beloved more than another beloved, that thou dost so charge us?

10 My beloved is white and ruddy, the chiefest among ten thousand.

11 His head is as the most fine gold, his locks are bushy, and black as a raven.

12 His eyes are as the eyes of doves by the rivers of waters, washed with milk, and fitly set.

13 His cheeks are as a bed of spices, as sweet flowers: his lips like lilies, dropping sweet smelling myrrh.

14 His hands are as gold rings set with the beryl: his belly is as bright ivory overlaid with sapphires.

15 His legs are as pillars of marble, set upon sockets of fine gold: his countenance is as Lebanon, excellent as the cedars.

16 His mouth is most sweet: yea, he is altogether lovely. This is my beloved, and this is my friend, O daughters of Jerusalem.

Chapter 6

1 Whither is thy beloved gone, O thou fairest among women? whither is thy beloved turned aside? that we may seek him with thee.

2 My beloved is gone down into his garden, to the beds of spices, to feed in the gardens, and to gather lilies.

3 I am my beloved's, and my beloved is mine: he feedeth among the lilies.

4 Thou art beautiful, O my love, as Tirzah, comely as Jerusalem, terrible as an army with banners.

5 Turn away thine eyes from me, for they have overcome me: thy hair is as a flock of goats that appear from Gilead.

6 Thy teeth are as a flock of sheep which go up from the washing, whereof every one beareth twins, and there is not one barren among them.

7 As a piece of a pomegranate are thy temples within thy locks.

8 There are threescore queens, and fourscore concubines, and virgins without number.

9 My dove, my undefiled is but one; she is the only one of her mother, she is the choice one of her that bare her. The daughters saw her, and blessed her; yea, the queens and the concubines, and they praised her.

10 Who is she that looketh forth as the morning, fair as the moon, clear as the sun, and terrible as an army with banners?

11 I went down into the garden of nuts to see the fruits of the valley, and to see whether the vine flourished and the pomegranates budded.

12 Or ever I was aware, my soul made me like the chariots of Amminadib.

13 Return, return, O Shulamite; return, return, that we may look upon thee. What will ye see in the Shulamite? As it were the company of two armies.

Chapter 7

1 How beautiful are thy feet with shoes, O prince's daughter! the joints of thy thighs are like jewels, the work of the hands of a cunning workman.

2 Thy navel is like a round goblet, which wanteth not liquor: thy belly is like an heap of wheat set about with lilies.

3 Thy two breasts are like two young roes that are twins.

4 Thy neck is as a tower of ivory; thine eyes like the fishpools in Heshbon, by the gate of Bathrabbim: thy nose is as the tower of Lebanon which looketh toward Damascus.

5 Thine head upon thee is like Carmel, and the hair of thine head like purple; the king is held in the galleries.

6 How fair and how pleasant art thou, O love, for delights! 7 This thy stature is like to a palm tree, and thy breasts to clusters of grapes.

8 I said, I will go up to the palm tree, I will take hold of the boughs thereof: now also thy breasts shall be as clusters of the vine, and the smell of thy nose like apples;

9 And the roof of thy mouth like the best wine for my beloved, that goeth down sweetly, causing the lips of those that are asleep to speak.

10 I am my beloved's, and his desire is toward me.

11 Come, my beloved, let us go forth into the field; let us lodge in the villages.

12 Let us get up early to the vineyards; let us see if the vine flourish, whether the tender grape appear, and the pomegranates bud forth: there will I give thee my loves.

13 The mandrakes give a smell, and at our gates are all manner of pleasant fruits, new and old, which I have laid up for thee, O my beloved.

Chapter 8

1 O that thou wert as my brother, that sucked the breasts of my mother! when I should find thee without, I would kiss thee; yea, I should not be despised.

2 I would lead thee, and bring thee into my mother's house, who would instruct me: I would cause thee to drink of spiced wine of the juice of my pomegranate.

3 His left hand should be under my head, and his right hand should embrace me.

4 I charge you, O daughters of Jerusalem, that ye stir not up, nor awake my love, until he please.

5 Who is this that cometh up from the wilderness, leaning upon her beloved? I raised thee up under the apple tree: there thy mother brought thee forth: there she brought thee forth that bare thee.

6 Set me as a seal upon thine heart, as a seal upon thine arm: for love is strong as death; jealousy is cruel as the grave: the coals thereof are coals of fire, which hath a most vehement flame.

7 Many waters cannot quench love, neither can the floods drown it: if a man would give all the substance of his house for love, it would utterly be contemned.

8 We have a little sister, and she hath no breasts: what shall we do for our sister in the day when she shall be spoken for?

9 If she be a wall, we will build upon her a palace of silver: and if she be a door, we will inclose her with boards of cedar.

10 I am a wall, and my breasts like towers: then was I in his eyes as one that found favour.

11 Solomon had a vineyard at Baalhamon; he let out the vineyard unto keepers; every one for the fruit thereof was to bring a thousand pieces of silver.

12 My vineyard, which is mine, is before me: thou, O Solomon, must have a thousand, and those that keep the fruit thereof two hundred.

13 Thou that dwellest in the gardens, the companions hearken to thy voice: cause me to hear it.

14 Make haste, my beloved, and be thou like to a roe or to a young hart upon the mountains of spices.

The Psalms of Solomon

(J. Rendel Harris Translation)

THIS collection of eighteen war songs are the gift of an ancient Semitic writer. The original manuscript has perished but fortunately Greek translations have been preserved, and recently a Syriac version of the same songs has turned up and was published in English for the first time in 1909 by Dr. Rendel Harris. The date of the writing may be established at the middle of the First Century B. C. because the theme of these songs is that of Pompey's actions in Palestine and his death in Egypt in 48 B. C.

These psalms had an important position and were widely circulated in the early Church. They are frequently referred to in the various Codexes and histories of the first few centuries of the Christian Era.

Later, they became lost through inexplicable reasons; and have only been recovered for our use after the lapse of many centuries. Besides the literary value of the trumpet-like rhythm of these verses, we have here a chapter of stirring ancient history written by an eyewitness. Pompey comes out of the West. He uses battering-rams on the fortifications. His soldiers defile the altar. He is slain in Egypt after a fearful career. In the "righteous" of these psalms we see the Pharisees; in the "sinners" we see the Sadducees. It is an epic of a great people in the throes of a great crisis.

Psalm 1

"They became insolent in their prosperity...."

I cried unto the Lord when I was in distress,
  Unto God when sinners assailed.
Suddenly the alarm of war was heard before me;
  I said, He will hearken to me for I am full of righteousness.
I thought in my heart that I was full of righteousness,
  Because I was well off and had become rich in children.
Their wealth spread to the whole earth,
  And their glory unto the end of the earth.
They were exalted unto the stars;
  They said they would never fan.
But they became insolent in their prosperity,
  And they were without understanding,
Their sins were in secret,
  And even I had no knowledge of them.
Their transgressions went beyond those of the heathen before them;
  They utterly polluted the holy things of the Lord.

Psalm 2

The desecration of Jerusalem; captivity, murder, and raping. A psalm of utter despair.

When the sinner waxed proud, with a battering-ram he cast down fortified walls,
  And thou didst not restrain him.
Alien nations ascended Thine altar,
  They trampled it proudly with their sandals;
Because the sons of Jerusalem had defiled the holy things of the Lord,
  Had profaned with iniquities the offerings of God.
Therefore He said: Cast them far from Me;

. . . . . .

It was set at naught before God,
  It was utterly dishonoured;
The sons and the daughters were m grievous captivity,
  Sealed was their neck, branded was it among the nations.

According to their sins hath He done unto them,
  For He hath left them in the hands of them that prevailed.
He hath turned away His face from pitying them,
  Young and old and their children together;
For they had done evil one and all, in not hearkening.
  And the heavens were angry,
And the earth abhorred them;

For no man upon it had done what they did,
And the earth recognized all
   Thy righteous judgements, O God.
They set the sons of Jerusalem to be mocked at in return for the harlots in her;
   Every wayfarer entered in in the full light of day.
They made mock with their transgressions, as they themselves were wont to do;
   In the full light of day they revealed their iniquities.
And the daughters of Jerusalem were defiled in accordance with Thy judgement,
   Because they had defiled themselves with unnatural intercourse.
I am pained in my bowels and my inward parts for these things.

And yet I will justify Thee, O God, in uprightness of heart,
   For in Thy judgements is Thy righteousness displayed, O God.
For Thou hast rendered to the sinners according to their deeds,
   Yea, according to their sins, which were very wicked.
Thou hast uncovered their sins, that Thy judgement might be manifest;
   Thou hast wiped out their memorial from the earth.
God is a righteous judge,
   And he is no respecter of persons.

For the nations reproached Jerusalem, trampling it down;
   Her beauty was dragged down from the throne of glory.

She girded on sackcloth instead of comely raiment,
  A rope was about her head instead of a crown.
She put off the glorious diadem which God had set upon her,
  In dishonour was her beauty cast upon the ground.

And I saw and entreated the Lord and said,
  Long enough, O Lord has Thine hand been heavy on Israel, in bringing the nations upon them.
For they have made sport unsparingly in wrath and fierce anger;
  And they will make an utter end, unless Thou, O Lord, rebuke them in Thy wrath.
For they have done. it not in zeal, but in lust of soul,
  Pouring out their wrath upon us with a view to rapine.
Delay not, O God, to recompense them on their heads,
  To turn the pride of the dragon into dishonour.
And I had not long to wait before God showed me the insolent one
  Slain on the mountains of Egypt,
  Esteemed of less account than the least, on land and sea;
His body, too, borne hither and thither on the billows with much insolence,
  With none to bury him, because He had rejected him with dishonour.

He reflected not that he was man,
  And reflected not on the latter end;
He said: I will be lord of land and sea;

And he recognized not that it is God who is great,
   Mighty in His great strength.
He is king over the heavens,
   And judgeth kings and kingdoms.
It is He who setteth me up in glory,
   And bringeth down the proud to eternal destruction in dishonour,
   Because they knew Him not.

And now behold, ye princes of the earth, the judgement of the Lord,
   For a great king and righteous is He, judging all that is under heaven.
Bless God, ye that fear the Lord with wisdom,
   For the mercy of the Lord will ~e upon them that fear Him, m the Judgement;
So that He will distinguish between the righteous and the sinner,
   And recompense the sinners for ever according to their deeds;
And have mercy on the righteous, delivering him from the affliction of the sinner,
   And recompensing the sinner for what he bath done to the righteous.
For the Lord is good to them that call upon Him in patience,
   Doing according to His mercy to His pious ones,
   Establishing them at all times before Him in strength.

Blessed be the Lord for ever before His servants.

Psalm 3

Righteousness versus Sin.

Why sleepest thou, O my soul,
   And blessest not the Lord?
Sing a new song,
   Unto God who is worthy to be praised.
Sing and be wakeful against His awaking,
   For good is a psalm sung to God from a glad heart.

The righteous remember the Lord at all times,
   With thanksgiving and declaration of the righteousness of the Lord's judgements.
The righteous despiseth not the chastening of the Lord;
   His will is always before the Lord.
The righteous stumbleth and holdeth the Lord righteous:
   He falleth and looketh out for what God will do to him;
He seeketh out whence his deliverance will come.
   The steadfastness of the righteous is from God, their deliverer;
There lodgeth not in the house of the righteous sin upon sin.
   The righteous continually searcheth his house,
To remove utterly all iniquity done by him in error.
   He maketh atonement for sins of ignorance by fasting and afflicting his soul,

And the Lord counteth guiltless every pious man and his house.
  The sinner stumbleth and curseth his life
The day when he was begotten, and his mother's travail.
  He addeth sins to sins, while he liveth;
He falleth--verily grievous is his fall--and riseth no more.
  The destruction of the sinner is for ever,
And he shall not be remembered, when the righteous is visited.
  This is the portion of sinners for ever.

But they that fear the Lord shall rise to life eternal,
  And their life shall be in the light of the Lord, and shall come to an end no more.

Psalm 4

A conversation of Solomon with the Men-pleasers.

Wherefore sittest thou, O profane man, in the council of the pious,
  Seeing that thy heart is far removed from the Lord,
  Provoking with transgressions the God of Israel?
Extravagant in speech, extravagant in outward seeming beyond all men,
  Is he that is severe of speech in condemning sinners in judgement.
And his hand is first upon him as though he acted in zeal,
  And yet he is himself guilty in respect of manifold sins and of

wantonness.

His eyes are upon every woman without distinction;
  His tongue lieth when he maketh contract with an oath.
By night and in secret he sinneth as though unseen,
  With his eyes he talketh to every woman of evil compacts.
He is swift to enter every house with cheerfulness as though guileless.

Let God remove those that live in hypocrisy in the company of the pious,
  Even the life of such an one with corruption of his flesh and penury.
Let God reveal the deeds of the men-pleasers,
  The deeds of such an one with laughter and derision;
That the pious may count righteous the judgement of their God,
  When sinners are removed from before the righteous,
  Even the man-pleaser who uttereth law guilefully.
And their eyes are fixed upon any man's house that is still secure,
  That they may, like the Serpent, destroy the wisdom of . . . with words of transgressors,
His words are deceitful that he may accomplish his wicked desire.
  He never ceaseth from scattering families as though they were orphans,
  Yea, he layeth waste a house on account of his lawless desire.
He deceiveth with words, saying, There is none that seeth, or judgeth.
He fills one house with lawlessness,

And then his eyes are fixed upon the next house,
  To destroy it with words that give wing to desire.
Yet with all these his soul like Sheol, is not sated.

Let his portion, O Lord, be dishonoured before thee;
  Let him go forth groaning, and come home cursed.
Let his life be spent in anguish, and penury, and want, O Lord;
  Let his sleep be beset with pains and his awaking with perplexities.
Let sleep be withdrawn from his eyelids at night;
  Let him fail dishonourably in every work of his hands.
Let him come home empty-handed to his house,
  And his house be void of everything wherewith he could sate his appetite.
Let his old age be spent in childless loneliness until his removal by death.

Let the flesh of the men-pleasers be rent by wild beasts,
  And let the bones of the lawless lie dishonoured in the sight of the sun.
Let ravens peck out the eyes of the hypocrites.
For they have laid waste many houses of men, in dishonour,
  And scattered them in their lust;
And they have not remembered God,
  Nor feared God in all these things;
  But they have provoked God's anger and vexed Him.

May He remove them from off the earth,

  Because with deceit they beguiled the souls of the flawless.

Blessed are they that fear the Lord in their flawlessness;

  The Lord shall deliver them from guileful men and sinners,

  And deliver us from every stumbling-block of the lawless (men).

Let God destroy them that insolently work all unrighteousness,

  For a great and mighty judge is the Lord our God in righteousness.

Let Thy mercy, O Lord, be upon all them that love Thee.

Psalm 5

A statement of the philosophy of the indestructibility of matter. One of the tenets of modern physics.

O Lord God, I will praise Thy name with joy,

  In the midst of them that know Thy righteous judgements.

For Thou art good and merciful, the refuge of the poor;

  When I cry to Thee, do not silently disregard me.

For no man taketh spoil from a mighty man;

  Who, then, can take aught of a that Thou hast made, except Thou Thyself givest?

For man and his portion lie before Thee in the balance;

  He cannot add to, so as to enlarge, what has been prescribed by Thee.

O God, when we are in distress we call upon Thee for help,
  And Thou dost not turn back our petition, for Thou art our God.
Cause not Thy hand to be heavy upon us,
  Lest through necessity we sin.
Even though Thou restore us not, we will not keep away;
  But unto Thee will we come.
For if I hunger, unto Thee will I cry, O God;
  And *Thou* wilt give to me.

Birds and fish dost Thou nourish,
  In that Thou givest rain to the steppes that green grass may spring up,
  So to prepare fodder in the steppe for every living thing;
And if they hunger, unto Thee do they lift up their face.
Kings and rulers and peoples *Thou* dost nourish, O God;
  And who is the help of the poor and needy, if not Thou, O Lord?
And Thou wilt hearken--for who is good and gentle but thou?--
  Making glad the soul of the humble by opening Thine hand in mercy.

Man's goodness is bestowed grudgingly and ...;
  And if he repeat it without murmuring, even that is marvellous.
But Thy gift is great in goodness and wealth,
  And he whose hope is set on Thee shall have no lack of gifts.
Upon the whole earth is Thy mercy, O Lord, in goodness.

Happy is he whom God remembereth in granting to him a due sufficiency;

  If a man abound overmuch, he sinneth.

Sufficient are moderate means with righteousness,

  And hereby the blessing of the Lord becomes abundance with righteousness.

They that fear the Lord rejoice in good gifts,

  And thy goodness is upon Israel in Thy kingdom.

Blessed is the glory of the Lord, for He is our king.

Psalm 6

A song of hope and fearlessness and peace.

Happy is the man whose heart is fixed to call upon the name of the Lord;

  When he remembereth the name of the Lord, he will be saved.

His ways are made even by the Lord,

  And the works of his hands are preserved by the Lord his God.

At what he sees in his bad dreams, his soul shall not be troubled;

  When he passes through rivers and the tossing of the seas, he shall not be dismayed.

He ariseth from his sleep, and blesseth the name of the Lord:

  When his heart is at peace, he singeth to the name of his God,

  And he entreateth the Lord for all his house.

And the Lord heareth the prayer of every one that feareth God,

And every request of the soul that hopes for Him doth the Lord accomplish.

Blessed is the Lord, who showeth mercy to those who love Him in sincerity.

Psalm 7

The fine old doctrine--"Thou art our Shield!"

Make not Thy dwelling afar from us, O God;
  Lest they assail us that hate us without cause.
For Thou hast rejected them, O God;
  Let not their foot trample upon Thy holy inheritance.
Chasten us Thyself in Thy good pleasure;
  But give us not up to the nations;
For, if Thou sendest pestilence,
  Thou Thyself givest it charge concerning us;
For Thou art merciful,
  And wilt not be angry to the point of consuming us.

While Thy name dwelleth in our midst, we shall find mercy;
  And the nations shall not prevail against us.
For Thou art our shield,
  And when we call upon Thee, Thou hearkenest to us;
For Thou wilt pity the seed of Israel for ever
  And Thou wilt not reject them:

But we shall, be under Thy yoke for ever,
   And under the rod of Thy chastening.
Thou wilt establish us in the time that Thou helpest us,
   Showing mercy to the house of Jacob on the day wherein Thou didst promise to help them.

Psalm 8

Some remarkable similes of war creeping on Jerusalem. A survey of the sins that brought all this trouble.

Distress and the sound of war hath my ear heard,
   The sound of a trumpet announcing slaughter and calamity,
The sound of much people as of an exceeding high wind,
   As a tempest with mighty fire sweeping through the Negeb.
And I said in my heart, Surely God judgeth us;
   A sound I hear moving towards Jerusalem, the holy city
My loins were broken at what I heard, my knees tottered;
   My heart was afraid, my bones were dismayed like flax.
I said: They establish their ways in righteousness.

I thought upon the judgments of God since the creation of heaven and earth;
   I held God righteous in His judgements which have been from of old.
God bare their sins in the full light of day;
   All the earth came to know the righteous judgements of God.

In secret places underground their iniquities were committed to provoke Him to anger;
They wrought confusion, son with mother and father with daughter;
  They committed adultery, every man with his neighhour's wife.
They concluded covenants with one another with an oath touching these things;
  They plundered the sanctuary of God, as though there was no avenger.
They trode the altar of the Lord, coming straight from all manner of uncleanness;
  And with menstrual blood they defiled the sacrifices, as though these were common flesh.
They left no sin undone, wherein they surpassed not the heathen.

Therefore God mingled for them a spirit of wandering;
  And gave them to drink a cup of undiluted wine, that they might become drunken.
He brought him that is from the end of the earth, that smiteth mightily;
  He decreed war against Jerusalem, and against her land.
The princes of the land went to meet him with joy: they said unto him:
  Blessed be thy way! Come ye, enter ye in with peace.
They made the rough ways even, before his entering in;
  They opened the gates to Jerusalem, they crowned its walls.

As a father entereth the house of his sons, so he entered Jerusalem in peace;

  He established his feet there in great safety.

He captured her fortresses and the wall of Jerusalem;

  For God Himself led him in safety, while they wandered.

He destroyed their princes and every one wise in counsel;

  He poured out the blood of the inhabitants of Jerusalem, like the water of uncleanness.

He led away their sons and daughters, whom they had begotten in defilement.

They did according to their uncleanness, even as their fathers had done:

  They defiled Jerusalem and the things that had been hallowed to the name of God.

But God hath shown Himself righteous in His judgements upon the nations of the earth;

  And the pious servants of God are like innocent lambs in their midst.

Worthy to be praised is the Lord that judgeth the whole earth in His righteousness.

Behold, now, O God, Thou hast shown us Thy judgement in Thy righteousness;

  Our eyes have seen Thy judgements, O God.

We have justified Thy name that is honoured for ever;

For Thou are the God of righteousness, judging Israel with chastening.

Turn, O God, Thy mercy upon us, and have pity upon us;
  Gather together the dispersed of Israel, with mercy and goodness;
For Thy faithfulness is with us,
And though we have stiffened our neck, yet Thou art our chastener;
  Overlook us not, O our God, lest the nations swallow us up, as though there were none to deliver.

But Thou art our God from the beginning,
  And upon Thee is our hope set, O Lord;
And we will not depart from Thee,
  For good are Thy judgements upon us.
Ours and our children's be Thy good pleasure for ever;
  O Lord, our Saviour, we shall never more be moved.
The Lord is worthy to be praised for His judgements with the mouth of His pious ones;
  And blessed be Israel of the Lord for ever.

Psalm 9

The exile of the tribes of Israel. A reference to the covenant which God made with Adam. (See the First Book of Adam and Eve, Chap. III, Verse 7).

When Israel was led away captive into a strange land,
  When they fell away from the Lord who redeemed them,
  They were cast away from the inheritance, which the Lord had given them.
Among every nation were the dispersed of Israel according to the word of God,
  That Thou mightest be justified, O God, in Thy righteousness by reason of our transgressions:
  For Thou art a just judge over all the peoples of the earth.
For from Thy knowledge none that doeth unjustly is hidden,
  And the righteous deeds of Thy pious ones are before Thee, O Lord;
  Where, then, can a man hide himself from Thy knowledge, O God?
Our works are subject to our own choice and power
  To do right or wrong in the works of our hands;
  And in Thy righteousness Thou visitest the sons of men.
He that doeth righteousness layeth up life for himself with the Lord;
  And he that doeth wrongly forfeits his life to destruction;
For the judgements of the Lord are given in righteousness to every

man and his house.

Unto whom art Thou good, O God, except to them that call upon the Lord?

He cleanseth from sins a soul when it maketh confession, when it maketh acknowledgement;

For shame is upon us and u on our faces on account of all these things.

And to whom doth He forgive sins, except to them that have sinned?

Thou blessest the righteous, and dost not reprove them for the sins that they have committed;

And Thy goodness is upon them that sin, when they repent.

And, now, Thou art our God, and we the people whom Thou hast loved:

Behold and show pity, O God of Israel, for we are Thine;

And remove not Thy mercy from us, lest they assail us.

For Thou didst choose the seed of Abraham before all the nations,

And didst set Thy name upon us, O Lord,

And Thou wilt not reject us for ever.

Thou madest a covenant with our fathers concerning us;

And we hope in Thee, when our soul turneth unto Thee.

The mercy of the Lord be upon the house of Israel for ever and ever.

Psalm 10

A glorious hymn. Further reference to the eternal covenant between God and Man.

Happy is the man whom the Lord remembereth with reproving,
  And whom He restraineth from the way of evil with strokes
    That he may be cleansed from sin, that it may not be multiplied.
He that maketh ready his back for strokes shall be cleansed,
  For the Lord is good to them that endure chastening.
For He maketh straight the ways of the righteous,
  And doth not pervert them by His chastening.
And the mercy of the Lord is upon them that love Him in truth,
  And the Lord remembereth His servants in mercy.
For the testimony is in the law of the eternal covenant,
  The testimony of the Lord is on the ways of men in His visitation.
Just and kind is our Lord in His judgements for ever,
  And Israel shall praise the name of the Lord in gladness.
And the pious shall give thanks in the assembly of the people;
  And on the poor shall God have mercy in the gladness of Israel;
For good and merciful is God for ever,
  And the assemblies of Israel shall glorify the name of the Lord.

The salvation of the Lord be upon the house of Israel unto everlasting gladness!

Psalm 11

Jerusalem hears a trumpet and stands on tiptoe to see her children returning from the North, East and West.

Blow ye in Zion on the trumpet to summon the saints,
  Cause ye to be heard in Jerusalem the voice of him that bringeth good tidings;
  For God hath had pity on Israel in visiting them.
Stand on the height, O Jerusalem, and behold thy children,
  From the East and the West, gathered together by the Lord;
From the North they come in the gladness of their God,
  From the isles afar off God hath gathered them.
High mountains hath He abased into a plain for them;
  The hills fled at their entrance.
The woods gave them shelter as they passed by;
  Every sweet-smelling tree God caused to spring up for them,
  That Israel might pass by in the visitation of the glory of their God.
Put on, O Jerusalem, thy glorious garments;
  Make ready thy holy robe;
  For God hath spoken good concerning Israel, for ever and ever.
Let the Lord do what He hath spoken concerning Israel and Jerusalem;
  Let the Lord raise up Israel by His glorious name.

The mercy of the Lord be upon Israel for ever and ever.

Psalm 12

An appeal for family tranquility and peace and quiet at home.

O Lord, deliver my soul from the lawless and wicked man,
  From the tongue that is lawless and slanderous, and speaketh lies and deceit.
Manifoldly twisted are the words of the tongue of the wicked man,
  Even as among a people a fire that burneth up their beauty.
So he delights to fill houses with a lying tongue,
  To cut down the trees of gladness which setteth on fire transgressors,
  To involve households in warfare by means of slanderous lips.

May God remove far from the innocent the lips of transgressors by bringing them to want
  And may the bones of slanderers be scattered far away from them that fear the Lord!
  In flaming fire perish the slanderous tongue far away from the pious!
May the Lord preserve the quiet soul that hateth the unrighteous;
  And may the Lord establish the man that followeth peace at home.
The salvation of the Lord be upon Israel His servant for ever;

And let the sinners perish together at the presence of the Lord;
But let the Lord's pious ones inherit the promises of the Lord.

Psalm 13

Of Solomon. A Psalm. Comfort for the righteous.

The right hand of the Lord hath covered me;
  The right hand of the Lord hath spared us.
The arm of the Lord hath saved us from the sword that passed through,
  From famine and the death of sinners.
Noisome beasts ran upon them:
  With their teeth they tore their flesh,
  And with their molars crushed their bones.
But from all these things the Lord delivered us.
The righteous was troubled on account of his errors,
  Lest he should be taken away along with the sinners;
For terrible is the overthrow of the sinner;
  But not one of all these things toucheth the righteous.
For not alike are the chastening of the righteous for sins done in ignorance,
  And the overthrow of the sinners.
Secretly is the righteous chastened,
  Lest the sinner rejoice over the righteous.
For He correcteth the righteous as a beloved son.

And his chastisement is as that of a first-born.
For the Lord spareth His pious ones,
  And blotteth out their errors by His chastening.
For the life of the righteous shall be for ever;
  But sinners shall be taken away into destruction,,
  And their memorial shall be found no more.
But upon the pious is the mercy of the Lord,
  And upon them that fear Him His mercy.

Psalm 14

Sinners "love the brief day spent in companionship with their sin."
Profound wisdom, beautifully expressed.

Faithful is the Lord to them that love Him in truth,
  To them that endure His chastening,
To them that walk in the righteousness of His commandments,
  In the law which He commanded us that we might live.
The pious of the Lord shall live by it for ever;
  The Paradise of the Lord, the trees of life, are His pious ones.
Their planting is rooted for ever;
  They shall not be plucked up all the days of heaven:
For the portion and the inheritance of God is Israel.
But not so are the sinners and transgressors,
  Who love the brief day spent in companionship with their sin;
Their delight is in fleeting corruption,
  And they remember not God.

For the ways of men are known before Him at all times,
  And He knoweth the secrets of the heart before they come to pass.
Therefore their inheritance is Sheol and darkness and destruction
  And they shall not be found in the day when the righteous obtain mercy;
But the pious of the Lord shall inherit life in gladness.

Psalm 15

The psalmist restates the great philosophy of Right and Wrong.

When I was in distress I called upon the name of the Lord,
  I hoped for the help of the God of Jacob and was saved;
  For the hope and refuge of the poor art Thou, O God.
For who, O God, is strong except to give thanks unto Thee in truth?
  And wherein is a man powerful except in giving thanks to Thy name?
A new psalm with song in gladness of heart,
  The fruit of the lips with the well-tuned instrument of the tongue,
  The first fruits of the lips from a pious and righteous heart--
He that offereth these things shall never be shaken by evil;
  The flame of fire and the wrath against the unrighteous shall not touch him,

When it goeth forth from the face of the Lord against sinners,
  To destroy all the substance of sinners,
For the mark of God is upon the righteous that they may be saved.

Famine and sword and pestilence shall be far from the righteous,
  For they shall flee away from the pious as men pursued in war;
But they shall pursue sinners and overtake them,
  And they that do lawlessness shall not escape the judgement of God;
As by enemies experienced in war shall they be overtaken,
  For the mark of destruction is upon their forehead.
And the inheritance of sinners is destruction and darkness,
  And their iniquities shall pursue them unto Sheol beneath.
Their inheritance shall not be found of their children,
  For sins shall lay waste the houses of sinners.
And sinners shall perish for ever in the day of the Lord's judgement,
  When God visiteth the earth with His judgement.
But they that fear the Lord shall find mercy therein,
  And shall live by the compassion of their God;
But sinners shall perish for ever.

Psalm 16

The psalmist again expresses profound truth
"For if Thou givest not strength,
who can endure chastisement?"

When my soul slumbered being afar from the Lord, I had all but slipped down to the pit,
   When I was far from God, my soul had been well-nigh poured out unto death,
I had been nigh unto the gates of Sheol with the sinner,
   When my soul departed from the Lord God of Israel--
Had not the Lord helped me with His everlasting mercy.

He pricked me, as a horse is pricked, that I might serve Him,
   My saviour and helper at all times saved me.
I will give thanks unto Thee, O God, for Thou hast helped me to my salvation;
   And hast not counted me with sinners to my destruction.
Remove not Thy mercy from me, O God,
   Nor Thy memorial from my heart until I die.
Rule me, O God, keeping me back from wicked sin,
   And from every wicked woman that causeth the simple to stumble.
And let not the beauty of a lawless woman beguile me,
   Nor any one that is subject to unprofitable sin.

Establish the works of my hands before Thee,
  And preserve my goings in the remembrance of Thee.
Protect my tongue and my lips with words of truth;
  Anger and unreasoning wrath put far from me.
Murmuring, and impatience in affliction, remove far from me
  When, if I sin, Thou chastenest me that I may return unto Thee.
But with goodwill and cheerfulness support my soul;
  When Thou strengthenest my soul, what is given to me will be sufficient for me.
For if *Thou* givest not strength,
Who can endure chastisement with poverty?
When a man is rebuked by means of his corruption,
  Thy testing of him is in his flesh and in the affliction of poverty.
If the righteous endureth in all these trials, he shall receive mercy from the Lord.

Psalm 17

"They set a worldly monarchy . . . . they lay waste the Throne of David!"
A poetic narrative about the utter disintegration of a great nation.

O Lord, Thou art our King for ever and ever,
  For in Thee, O God, doth our soul glory.
How long are the days of man's life upon the earth?
  As are his days, so is the hope set upon him.
But *we* hope in God, our deliverer;
For the might of our God is for ever with mercy,

And the kingdom of our God is for ever over the nations in judgement.

Thou, O Lord, didst choose David to be king over Israel,
  And swaredst to him touching his seed that never should his kingdom fail before Thee.
But, for our sins, sinners rose up against us;
  They assailed us and thrust us out;
  What Thou hadst not promised to them, they took away from us with violence.
They in no wise glorified Thy honourable name;
  They set a worldly monarchy in place of that which was their excellency;
  They laid waste the throne of David in tumultuous arrogance.
But Thou, O God, didst cast them down, and remove their seed from the earth,
  In that there rose up against them a man that was alien to our race.
According to their sins didst Thou recompense them, O God;
  So that it befell them according to their deeds.
God showed them no pity;
  He sought out their seed and let not one of them go free.
Faithful is the Lord in all His judgements
  Which He doeth upon the earth.

The lawless one laid waste our land so that none inhabited it,
  They destroyed young and old and their children together.
In the heat of His anger He sent them away even unto the west,
  And He exposed the rulers of the land unsparingly to derision.
Being an alien the enemy acted proudly,
  And his heart was alien from Our God.
And all things whatsoever he did in Jerusalem,
  As also the nations in the cities to their gods.

And the children of the covenant in the midst of the mingled peoples surpassed them in evil.
  There was not among them one that wrought in the midst of Jerusalem mercy and truth.
They that loved the synagogues of the pious fled from them,
  As sparrows that fly from their nest.
They wandered in deserts that their lives might be saved from harm,
  And precious in the eyes of them that lived abroad was any that escaped alive from them.
  Over the whole earth were they scattered by lawless men.
For the heavens withheld the rain from dropping upon the earth,
  Springs were stopped that sprang perennially out of the deeps, that ran down from lofty mountains.
For there was none among them that wrought righteousness and justice;
  From the chief of them to the least of them all were sinful;
  The king was a transgressor, and the judge disobedient, and the

people sinful.
Behold, O Lord, and raise up unto them their king, the son of David,
   At the time in the which Thou seest, O God, that he may reign over Israel Thy servant.
And gird him with strength, that he may shatter unrighteous rulers,
   And that he may purge Jerusalem from nations that trample her down to destruction.
Wisely, righteously he shall thrust out sinners from the inheritance,
   He shall destroy the pride of the sinner as a potter's vessel.
With a rod of iron he shall break in pieces all their substance,
   He shall destroy the godless nations with the word of his mouth;
At his rebuke nations shall flee before him,
   And he shall reprove sinners for the thoughts of their heart.

And he shall gather together a holy people, whom he shall lead in righteousness,
   And he shall judge the tribes of the people that has been sanctified by the Lord his God.
And he shall not suffer unrighteousness to lodge any more in their midst,
   Nor shall there dwell with them any man that knoweth wickedness,
   For he shall know them, that they are all sons of their God.

And he shall divide them according to their tribes upon the land,
  And neither sojourner nor alien shall sojourn with them any more.
He shall judge peoples and nations in the wisdom of his righteousness. *Selah*.

And he shall have the heathen nations to serve him under his yoke;
  And he shall glorify the Lord in a place to be seen of all the earth;
  And he shall purge Jerusalem, making it holy as of old:
So that nations shall come from the ends of the earth to see his glory,
  Bringing as gifts her sons who had fainted.
  And to see the glory of the Lord, wherewith God hath glorified her.
And he shall be a righteous king, taught of God, over them,
And there shall be no unrighteousness in his days in their midst,
  For all shall be holy and their king the anointed of the Lord.
For he shall not put his trust in horse and rider and bow,
  Nor shall he multiply for himself gold and silver for war,

Nor shall he gather confidence from a multitude for the day of battle.
The Lord Himself is his king, the hope of him that is mighty through his hope in God.

All nations shall be in fear before him,
  For he will smite the earth with the word of his mouth for ever.

He will bless the people of the Lord with wisdom and gladness,

And he himself will be pure from sin, so that he may rule a great people.

He will rebuke rulers, and remove sinners by the might of his word;

And relying upon his God, throughout his days he will not stumble;

For God will make him mighty by means of His holy spirit,

And wise by means of the spirit of understanding, with strength and righteousness.

And the blessing of the Lord will be with him: he will be strong and stumble not;

His hope will be in the Lord: who then can prevail against him?

He will, be mighty in his works, and strong in the fear of God,

He will be shepherding the flock of the Lord faithfully and righteously,

And will suffer none among them to stumble in their pasture.

He will lead them all aright,

And there will be no pride among them that any among them should be oppressed.

This will be the majesty of the king of Israel whom God knoweth;

He will raise him up over the house of Israel to correct him.

His words shall be more refined than costly gold, the choicest;

In the assemblies he will judge the peoples, the tribes of the sanctified.

His words shall be like the words of the holy ones in the midst of sanctified peoples.

Blessed be they that shall be in those days,
   In that they shall see the good fortune of Israel which God shall bring to pass in the gathering together of the tribes.

May the Lord hasten His mercy upon Israel!
   May He deliver us from the uncleanness of unholy enemies!

The Lord Himself is our king for ever and ever.

Psalm 18

With this psalm end the warlike Songs of Solomon.

Lord, Thy mercy is over the works of Thy hands for ever;
   Thy goodness is over Israel with a rich gift.

Thine eyes look upon them, so that none of them suffers want;
   Thine ears listen to the hopeful prayer of the poor.

Thy judgements are executed upon the whole earth in mercy;
   And Thy love is toward the seed of Abraham, the children of Israel.

Thy chastisement is upon us as upon a first-born, only-begotten son,
   To turn back the obedient soul from folly that is wrought in ignorance.

May God cleanse Israel against the day of mercy and blessing,
   Against the day of choice when

Blessed shall they be that shall be in those days,
   He bringeth back His anointed.

In that they shall see the goodness of the Lord which He shall perform for the generation that is to come,
Under the rod of chastening of the Lord's anointed in the fear of his God,
  In the spirit of wisdom and righteousness and strength;
That he may direct every man in the works of righteousness by the fear of God,
  That he may establish them all before the Lord,
  A good generation living in the fear of God in the days of mercy. Selah.

Great is our God and glorious, dwelling in the highest.
It is He who hath established in their courses the lights of heaven for determining seasons from year to year,
  And they have not turned aside from the way which He appointed them.
In the fear of God they pursue their path every day,
  From the day God created them and for evermore.
And they have erred not since the day He created them.
  Since the generations of old they have not withdrawn from their path,
  Unless God commanded them so to do by the command of His servants.

The Odes of Solomon

(J. Rendel Harris Translation)

HERE are some of the most beautiful songs of peace and joy that the world possesses. Yet their origin, the date of their writing, and the exact meaning of many of the verses remain one of the great literary mysteries.

They have come down to us in a single and very ancient document in Syriac language. Evidently that document is a translation from the original Greek. Critical debate has raged around these Odes; one of the most plausible explanations is that they are songs of newly baptized Christians of the First Century.

They are strangely lacking in historical allusions. Their radiance is no reflection of other days. They do not borrow from either the Old Testament or the Gospels. The inspiration of these verses is first-hand. They remind you of Aristides' remark, "*A new people with whom something Divine is mingled.*" Here is vigor and insight to which we can find parallels only in the most exalted parts of the Scriptures.

For these dazzling mystery odes, we owe our translation to J. Rendel Harris, MA., Hon. Fellow of Clare College, Cambridge. He says about them: "There does not seem to be anything about which everyone seem agreed unless it be that the Odes are of singular beauty and high spiritual value."

ODE 1

1 The Lord is on my head like a crown, and I shall not be without Him.
2 They wove for me a crown of truth, and it caused thy branches to bud in me.
3 For it is not like a withered crown which buddeth not: but thou livest upon my head, and thou hast blossomed upon my head.
4 Thy fruits are full-grown and perfect, they are full of thy salvation.

ODE 2

(*No part of this Ode has ever been identified.*)

ODE 3

The first words of this Ode have disappeared.

1 . . . I put on:
2 And his members are with him. And on them do I stand, and He loves me:
3 For I should not have known how to love the Lord, if He had not

loved me.

4 For who is able to distinguish love, except the one that is loved?

5 I love the Beloved, and my soul loves Him:

6 And where His rest is, there also am I;

7 And I shall be no stranger, for with the Lord Most High and Merciful there is no grudging.

8 I have been united to I-run, for the Lover has found the Beloved,

9 And because I shall love Him that, is the Son, I shall become a son;

10 For he that is joined to Him that is immortal, will also himself become immortal;

11 And he who has pleasure in the Living One, will become living.

12 This is the Spirit of the Lord, which doth not lie, which teacheth the sons of men to know His ways.

13 Be wise and understanding and vigilant. Hallelujah.

ODE 4

This Ode is important because of the historical allusion with which it commences. This may refer to the closing of the temple at Leontopolis in Egypt which would date this writing about 73 A. D.

1 No man, O my God, changeth thy holy place;

2 And it is not (possible) that he should change it and put it in another place: because he hath no power over it:

3 For thy sanctuary thou hast designed before thou didst make (other) places:

4 That which is the older shall not be altered by those that are younger

than itself.

5 Thou has given thy heart, O Lord, to thy believers: never wilt thou fail, nor be without fruits:

6 For one hour of thy Faith is more precious than all days and years.

7 For who is there that shall put on thy grace, and be hurt?

8 For thy seal is known: and thy creatures know it: and thy (heavenly) hosts possess it: and the elect archangels are clad with it.

9 Thou hast given us thy fellowship: it was not that thou wast in need of us: but that we are in need of thee:

10 Distill thy dews upon us and open thy rich fountains that pour forth to us milk and honey:

11 For there is no repentance with thee that thou shouldest repent of anything that thou hast promised:

12 And the end was revealed before thee: for what thou gavest, thou gavest freely:

13 So that thou mayest, not draw them back and take them again:

14 For all was revealed before thee as God, and ordered from the beginning before thee: and thou, O God, hast made all things. Hallelujah.

ODE 5

This Ode has strangely appeared in a speech by Salome in another ancient work called the Pistis Sophia.

1 I will give thanks unto thee, O Lord, because I love thee;
2 O Most High, thou wilt not forsake me, for thou art my hope:
3 Freely I have received thy grace, I shall live thereby:
4 My persecutors will come and not see me:
5 A cloud of darkness shall fall on their eyes; and an air of thick gloom shall darken them:
6 And they shall have no light to see: they may not take hold upon me.
7 Let their counsel become thick darkness, and what I have cunningly devised, let it return upon their own heads:
8 For they have devised a counsel, and it did not succeed:
9 For my hope is upon the Lord, and I will not fear, and because the Lord is my salvation, I will not fear:
10 And He is as a garland on my head and I shall not be moved; even if everything should be shaken, I stand firm;
11 And if all things visible should perish, I shall not die; because the Lord is with me and I am with Him. Hallelujah.

ODE 6

First century universalism is revealed in an interesting way in verse 10.

1 As the hand moves over the harp, and the strings speak.
2 So speaks in my members the Spirit of the Lord, and I speak by His love.
3 For it destroys what is foreign, and everything that is bitter:
4 For thus it was from the beginning and will be to the end, that nothing should be His adversary, and nothing should stand up against Him.
5 The Lord has multiplied the knowledge of Himself, and is zealous that these things should be known, which by His grace have been given to us.
6 And the praise of His name He gave us: our spirits praise His holy Spirit.
7 For there went forth a stream and became a river great and broad;
8 For it flooded and broke up everything and it brought (water) to the Temple:
9 And the restrainers of the children of men were not able to restrain it, nor the arts of those whose business it is to restrain waters;
10 For it spread over the face of the whole earth, and filled everything: and all the thirsty upon earth were given to drink of it;
11 And thirst was relieved and quenched: for from the Most High the draught was given.
12 Blessed then are the ministers of that draught who are entrusted

with that water of His:

13 They have assuaged the dry lips, and the will that had fainted they have raised up;

14 And souls that were near departing they have caught back from death:

15 And limbs that had fallen they straightened and set up:

16 They gave strength for their feebleness and light to their eyes:

17 For everyone knew them in the Lord, and they lived by the water of life for ever. Hallelujah.

ODE 7

A wonderfully, simple and joyful psalm on the Incarnation.

1 As the impulse of anger against evil, so is the impulse of joy over what is lovely, and brings in of its fruits without restraint:

2 My joy is the Lord and my impulse is toward Him: this path of mine is excellent:

3 For I have a helper, the Lord.

4 He hath caused me to know Himself, without grudging, by His simplicity: His kindness has humbled His greatness.

5 He became like me, in order that I might receive Him:

6 He was reckoned like myself in order that I might put Him on;

7 And I trembled not when I saw Him: because He was gracious to me:

8 Like my nature He became that I might learn Him and like my form, that I might not turn back from Him:

9 The Father of knowledge is the word of knowledge:

10 He who created wisdom is wiser than His works:

11 And He who created me when yet I was not knew what I should do when I came into being:

12 Wherefore He pitied me in His abundant grace: and granted me to ask from Him and to receive from His sacrifice:

13 Because He it is that is incorrupt, the fulness of the ages and the Father of them.

14 He hath given Him to be seen of them that are His, in order that they may recognize Him that made them: and that they might not suppose that they came of themselves:

15 For knowledge He hath appointed as its way, He hath widened it and extended it; and brought to all perfection;

16 And set over it the traces of His light, and I walked therein from the beginning even to the end.

17 For by Him it was wrought, and He was resting in the Son, and for its salvation He will take hold of everything;

18 And the Most High shall be known in His Saints, to announce to those that have songs of the coming of the Lord;

19 That they may go forth to meet Him, and may sing to Him with joy and with the harp of many tones:

20 The seers shall come before Him and they shall be seen before Him,

21 And they shall praise the Lord for His love: because He is near and beholdeth.

22 And hatred shall be taken from the earth, and along with jealousy it

shall be drowned:

23 For ignorance hath been destroyed, because the knowledge of the Lord hath arrived.

24 They who make songs shall sing the grace of the Lord Most High;

25 And they shall bring their songs, and their heart shall be like the day: and like the excellent beauty of the Lord their pleasant song:

26 And there shall neither be anything that breathes without knowledge, nor any that is dumb:

27 For He hath given a mouth to His creation, to open the voice of the mouth towards Him, to praise Him:

28 Confess ye His power, and show forth His grace. Hallelujah.

ODE 8

Note the sudden transition from the person of the Psalmist to the person of the Lord (v. 10). This is like the canonical Psalter in style.

1 Open ye, open ye your hearts to the exultation of the Lord:

2 And let your love be multiplied from the heart and even to the lips,

3 To bring forth fruit to the Lord [fruit], holy [fruit], and to talk with watchfulness in His light.

4 Rise up, and stand erect, ye who sometime were brought low:

5 Tell forth ye who were in silence, that your mouth hath been opened.

6 Ye, therefore, that were despised, be henceforth lifted up, because your righteousness hath been exalted.

7 For the right hand of the Lord is with you: and He is your helper:

8 And peace was prepared for you, before ever your war was.

9 Hear the word of truth, and receive the knowledge of the Most High.

10 Your flesh has not known what I am saying to you neither have your hearts known what I am showing to you.

11 Keep my secret, ye who are kept by it:

12 Keep my faith, ye who are kept by it.

13 And understand my knowledge, ye who know me in truth.

14 Love me with affection, ye who love:

15 For I do not turn away my face from them that are mine;

16 For I know them, and before they came into being I took knowledge of them, and on their faces I set my seal:

17 I fashioned their members: my own breasts I prepared for them, that they might drink my holy milk and live thereby.

18 I took pleasure in them and am not ashamed of them:

19 For my workmanship are they and the strength of my thoughts:

20 Who then shall rise up against my handiwork, or who is there that is not subject to them?

21 I willed and fashioned mind and heart: and they are mine, and by my own right hand I set my elect ones:

22 And my righteousness goeth before them and they shall not be deprived of my name, for it is with them.

23 Ask, and abound and abide in the love of the Lord,

24 And yet beloved ones in the Beloved: those who are kept, in Him that liveth:

25 And they that are saved in Him that was saved;

26 And ye shall be found incorrupt in all ages to the name of your Father. Hallelujah.

ODE 9

We shall never know surely whether the wars referred to here are spiritual or actual outward wars.

1 Open your ears and I will speak to you. Give me your souls that I may also give you my soul,
2 The word of the Lord and His good pleasures, the holy thought which He has devised concerning his Messiah.
3 For in the will of the Lord is your salvation, and His thought is everlasting life; and your end is immortality.
q Be enriched in God the Father, and receive the thought of the Most High.
5 Be strong and be redeemed by His grace.
6 For I announce to you peace, to you His saints;
7 That none of those who hear may fall in war, and that those again who have known Him may not perish, and that those who receive may not be ashamed.
8 An everlasting crown for ever is Truth. Blessed are they who set it on their heads:
9 A stone of great price is it; and there have been wars on account of the crown.
10 And righteousness hath taken it and hath given it to you.
11 Put on the crown in the true covenant of the Lord.

12 And all those who have conquered shall be written in His book.
13 For their book is victory which is yours. And she (Victory) sees you before her and wills that you shall be saved. Hallelujah.

ODE 10

A vigorous little Ode in which Christ Himself is the speaker.

1 The Lord hath directed my mouth by His word: and He hath opened my heart by His light: and He hath caused to dwell in me His deathless life;
2 And gave me that I might speak the fruit of His peace:
3 To convert the souls of them who are willing to come to Him; and to lead captive a good captivity for freedom.
4 I was strengthened and made mighty and took the world captive;
5 And it became to me for the praise of the Most High, and of God my Father.
6 And the Gentiles were gathered together who were scattered abroad.
7 And I was unpolluted by my love for them, because they confessed me in high places: and the traces of the light were set upon their heart:
8 And they walked in my life and were saved and became my people for ever and ever. Hallelujah.

ODE 11

A beautiful sketch of Paradise regained and the blessedness of those who have returned to the privileges of the fallen Adam.

1 My heart was cloven and its flower appeared; and grace sprang up in it: and it brought forth fruit to the Lord,

2 For the Most High clave my heart by His Holy Spirit and searched my affection towards Him: and filled me with His love.

3 And His opening of me became my salvation; and I ran in His way in His peace, even in the way of truth:

4 From the beginning and even to the end I acquired His knowledge:

5 And I was established upon the rock of truth, where He had set me up:

6 And speaking waters touched my lips from the fountain of the Lord plenteously:

7 And I drank and was inebriated with the living water that doth not die;

8 And my inebriation was not one without knowledge, but I forsook vanity and turned to the Most High my God,

9 And I was enriched by His bounty, and I forsook the folly which is diffused over the earth; and I stripped it off and cast it from me:

10 And the Lord renewed me in His raiment, and possessed me by His light, and from above He gave me rest in incorruption;

11 And I became like the land which blossoms and rejoices in its fruits:

12 And the Lord was like the sun shining on the face of the land;

13 He lightened my eyes, and my face received the dew; and my nostrils enjoyed the pleasant odour of the Lord;

14 And He carried me to His Paradise; where is the abundance of the pleasure of the Lord;

15 And I worshipped the Lord on account of His glory; and I said, Blessed, O Lord, are they who are planted in thy land! and those who have a place in thy Paradise;

16 And they grow by the fruits of the trees. And they have changed from darkness to light.

17 Behold! all thy servants are fair, who do good works, and turn away from wickedness to the pleasantness that is thine:

18 And they have turned back the bitterness of the trees from them, when they were planted in thy, land;

19 And everything became like a relic of thyself, and memorial for ever of thy faithful works.

20 For there is abundant room in thy Paradise, and nothing is useless therein;

21 But everything is filled with fruit; glory be to thee, O God, the delight of Paradise for ever. Hallelujah.

ODE 12

An exceptionally high level of spiritual thought.

1 He hath filled me with words of truth; that I may speak the same;

2 And like the flow of waters flows truth from my mouth, and my lips show forth His fruit.

3 And He has caused His knowledge to abound in me, because the mouth of the Lord is the true Word, and the door of His light;

4 And the Most High hath given it to His words, which are the interpreters of His own beauty, and the repeaters of His praise, and the confessors of His counsel, and the heralds of His thought, and the chasteners of His servants.

5 For the swiftness of the Word is inexpressible, and like its expression is its swiftness and force;

6 And its course knows no limit. Never doth it fail, but it stands sure, and it knows not descent nor the way of it.

7 For as its work is, so is its end: for it is light and the dawning of thought;

8 And by it the worlds talk one to the other; and in the Word there were those that were silent;

9 And from it came love and concord; and they spake one to the other whatever was theirs; and they were penetrated by the Word;

10 And they knew Him who made them, because they were in concord; for the mouth of the Most High spake to them; and His explanation ran by means of it:

11 For the dwelling-place of the Word is man: and its truth is love.

12 Blessed are they who by means thereof have understood everything, and have known the Lord in His truth. Hallelujah.

ODE 13

A strange little Ode.

1 Behold! the Lord is our mirror: open the eyes and see them in Him: and learn the manner of your face:
2 And tell forth praise to His spirit: and wipe off the filth from your face: and love His holiness and clothe yourselves therewith:
3 And be without stain at all times before Him. Hallelujah.

ODE 14

This Ode is as beautiful in style as the canonical Psalter.

1 As the eyes of a son to his father, so are my eyes, O Lord, at all times towards thee.
2 For with thee are my consolations and my delight.
3 Turn not away thy mercies from me, O Lord: and take not thy kindness from me.
4 Stretch out to me, O Lord, at all times thy right hand: and be my guide even unto the end, according to thy good pleasure.
5 Let me be well-pleasing before thee, because of thy glory and because of thy name:
6 Let me be preserved from evil, and let thy meekness, O Lord, abide

with me, and the fruits of thy love.

7 Teach me the Psalms of thy truth, that I may bring forth fruit in thee:

8 And open to me the harp of thy Holy Spirit, that with all its notes I may praise thee, O Lord.

9 And according to the multitude of thy tender mercies, so thou shalt give to me; and hasten to grant our petitions; and thou art able for all our needs. Hallelujah.

ODE 15

One of the loveliest Odes in this unusual collection.

1 As the sun is the joy to them that seek for its daybreak, so is my joy the Lord;

2 Because He is my Sun and His rays have lifted me up; and His light hath dispelled all darkness from my face.

3 In Him I have acquired eyes and have seen His holy day:

4 Ears have become mine and I have heard His truth.

5 The thought of knowledge hath been mine, and I have been delighted through Him.

6 The way of error I have left, and have walked towards Him and have received salvation from Him, without grudging.

7 And according to His bounty He hath given to me, and according to His excellent beauty He hath made me.

8 I have put on incorruption through His name: and have put oft corruption by His grace.

9 Death hath been destroyed before my face: and Sheol hath been abolished by my word:

10 And there hath gone up deathless life in the Lord's land,

11 And it hath been made known to His faithful ones, and hath been given without stint to all those that trust in Him. Hallelujah.

ODE 16

The beauty of God's creation.

1 As the work of the husbandman is the ploughshare: and the work of the steersman is the guidance of the ship:

2 So also my work is the Psalm of the Lord: my craft and my occupation are in His praises:

3 Because His love bath nourished my heart, and even to my lips His fruits He poured out.

4 For my love is the Lord, and therefore I will sing unto Him:

5 For I am made strong in His praise, and I have faith in Him.

6 I will open my mouth and His spirit will utter in me the glory of the Lord and His beauty; the work of His hands and the operation of His fingers:

7 The multitude of His mercies and the strength of His word.

8 For the word of the Lord searches out all things, both the invisible and that which reveals His thought;

9 For the eye sees His works, and the ear hears His thought;

10 He spread out the earth and He settled the waters in the sea:

11 He measured the heavens and fixed the stars: and He established the creation and set it up:

12 And He rested from His works:

13 And created things run in their courses, and do their works:

14 And they know not how to stand and be idle; and His heavenly hosts are subject to His word.

15 The treasure-chamber of the light is the sun, and the treasury of the darkness is the night:

16 And He made the sun for the day that it may be bright, but night brings darkness over the face of the land;

17 And their alternations one to the other speak the beauty of God:

IS And there is nothing that is without the Lord; for He was before any thing came into being:

19 And the worlds were made by His word, and by the thought of His heart. Glory and honour to His name. Hallelujah.

ODE 17

A peculiar change of personality, scarcely realized until the return from it in the last verse.

1 I was crowned by my God: my crown is living:

2 And I was justified in my Lord: my incorruptible salvation is He.

3 I was loosed from vanity, and I was not condemned:

4 The choking bonds were cut off by her hands: I received the face and the fashion of a new person: and I walked in it and was saved;

5 And the thought of truth led me on. And I walked after it and did

not wander:

6 And all that have seen me were amazed: and I was regarded by them as a strange person:

7 And He who knew and brought me up is the Most High in all His perfection. And He glorified me by His kindness, and raised my thoughts to the height of His truth.

8 And from thence He gave me the way of His precepts and I opened the doors that were closed,

9 And brake in pieces the bars of iron; but my iron melted and dissolved before me;

10 Nothing appeared closed to me: because I was the door of everything.

11 And I went over all my bondmen to loose them; that I might not leave any man bound or binding:

12 And I imparted my knowledge without grudging: and my prayer was in my love:

13 And I sowed my fruits in hearts, and transformed them into myself: and they received my blessing and lived;

14 And they were gathered to me and were saved; because they were to me as my own members and I was their head. Glory to thee our head, the Lord Messiah. Hallelujah.

ODE 18

A man who had a spiritual experience brings a message.

1 My heart was lifted up in the love of the Most High and was enlarged: that I might praise Him for His name's sake.
2 My members were strengthened that they might not fall from His strength.
3 Sicknesses removed from my body, and it stood to the Lord by His will. For His kingdom is true.
4 O Lord, for the sake of them that are deficient do not remove thy word from me!
5 Neither for the sake of their works do thou restrain from me thy perfection!
6 Let not the luminary be conquered by the darkness; nor let truth flee away from falsehood.
7 Thou wilt appoint me to victory; our Salvation is thy right hand. And thou wilt receive men from all quarters.
8 And thou wilt preserve whosoever is held in evils:
9 Thou art my God. Falsehood and death are not in thy mouth:
10 For thy will is perfection; and vanity thou knowest not,
11 Nor does it know thee.
12 And error thou knowest not,
13 Neither does it know thee.
14 And ignorance appeared like a blind man; and like the foam of the sea,
15 And they supposed of that vain thing that it was something great;

16 And they too came in likeness of it and became vain; and those have understood who have known and meditated;
17 And they have not been corrupt in their imagination; for such were in the mind of the Lord;
18 And they mocked at them that were walking in error;
19 And they spake truth from the inspiration which the Most High breathed into them; Praise and great comeliness to His name Hallelujah.

ODE 19

Fantastic and not in harmony with the other Odes. The reference to a painless Virgin Birth is notable.

1 A cup of milk was offered to me: and I drank it in the sweetness of the delight of the Lord.
2 The Son is the cup, and He who was milked is the Father:
3 And the Holy Spirit milked Him: because His breasts were full, and it was necessary for Him that His milk should be sufficiently released;
4 And the Holy Spirit opened His bosom and mingled the milk from the two breasts of the Father; and gave the mixture to the world without their knowing:
5 And they who receive in its fulness are the ones on the right hand.
6 The Spirit opened the womb of the Virgin and she received conception and brought forth; and the Virgin became a Mother with many mercies;

7 And she travailed and brought forth a Son, without incurring pain;

8 And because she was not sufficiently prepared, and she had not sought a midwife (for He brought her to bear) she brought forth, as if she were a man, of her own will;

9 And she brought Him forth openly, and acquired Him with great dignity,

10 And loved Him in His swaddling clothes and guarded Him kindly, and showed Him in Majesty. Hallelujah.

ODE 20

A mixture of ethics and mysticism; of the golden rule and the tree of life.

1 I am a priest of the Lord, and to Him I do priestly service: and to Him I offer the sacrifice of His thought.

2 For His thought is not like the thought of the world nor the thought of the flesh, nor like them that serve carnally.

3 The sacrifice of the Lord is righteousness, and purity of heart and lips.

4 Present your reins before Him blamelessly: and let not thy heart do violence to heart, nor thy soul to soul.

5 Thou shalt not acquire a stranger by the price of thy silver, neither shalt thou seek to devour thy neighbour,

6 Neither shalt thou deprive him of the covering of his nakedness.

7 But put on the grace of the Lord without stint; and come into His Paradise and make thee a garland from its tree,

8 And put it on thy head and be glad; and recline on His rest, and

glory shall go before thee,

9 And thou shalt receive of His kindness and of His grace; and thou shalt be flourishing in truth in the praise of His holiness. Praise and honour be to His name. Hallelujah.

ODE 21

A remarkable explanation of the "coats of skin" in the third chapter of Genesis.

1 My arms I lifted up to the Most High, even to the grace of the Lord: because He had cast off my bonds from me: and my Helper had lifted me up to His grace and to His salvation:
2 And I put off darkness and clothed myself with light,
3 And my soul acquired a body free from sorrow or affliction or pains.
4 And increasingly helpful to me was the thought of the Lord, and His fellowship in incorruption:
5 And I was lifted up in His light; and I served before Him,
6 And I became near to Him, praising and confessing Him;
7 My heart ran over and was found in my mouth: and it arose upon my lips; and the exultation of the Lord increased on my face, and His praise likewise. Hallelujah.

ODE 22

Like the Psalms of David in their exultation because of freedom.

1 He who brought me down from on high, also brought me up from the regions below;

2 And He who gathers together the things that are betwixt is He also who cast me down:

3 He who scattered my enemies had existed from ancient and my adversaries:

4 He who gave me authority over bonds that I might loose them;

5 He that overthrew by my hands the dragon with seven heads: and thou hast set me over his roots that I might destroy his seed.

6 Thou wast there and didst help me, and in every place thy name was a rampart me

7 Thy right hand destroyed his wicked poison; and thy hand levelled the way for those who believe in thee.

8 And thou didst choose them from the graves and didst separate them from the dead.

9 Thou didst take dead bones and didst cover them with bodies.

10 They were motionless, and thou didst give them energy for life.

11 Thy way was without corruption, and thy face; thou didst bring thy world to corruption: that everything might be dissolved, and then renewed,

12 And that the foundation for everything might be thy rock: and on it thou didst build thy kingdom; and it became the dwelling place of the saints. Hallelujah.

ODE 23

The reference to the sealed document sent by God is one of the great mysteries of the collection.

1 Joy is of the saints! and who shall put it on, but they alone?
2 Grace is of the elect! and who shall receive it except those who trust in it from the beginning?
3 Love is of the elect? And who shall put it on except those who have possessed it from the beginning?
4 Walk ye in the knowledge of the Most High without grudging: to His exultation and to the perfection of His knowledge.
5 And His thought was like a letter; His will descended from on high, and it was sent like an arrow which is violently shot from the bow:
6 And many hands rushed to the letter to seize it and to take and read it:
7 And it escaped their fingers and they were affrighted at it and at the seal that was upon it.
8 Because it was not permitted to them to loose its seal: for the power that was over the seal was greater than they.
9 But those who saw it went after the letter that they might know where it would alight, and who should read it and who should hear it.
10 But a wheel received it and came over it:
11 And there was with it a sign of the Kingdom and of the Government:
12 And everything which tried to move the wheel it mowed and cut

down:

13 And it gathered the multitude of adversaries, and bridged the rivers and crossed over and rooted up many forests and made a broad path.

14 The head went down to the feet, for down to the feet ran the wheel, and that which was a sign upon it.

15 The letter was one of command, for there were included in it all districts;

16 And there was seen at its head, the head which was revealed even the Son of Truth from the Most High Father,

17 And He inherited and took possession of everything. And the thought of many was brought to nought.

18 And all the apostates hasted and fled away. And those who persecuted and were enraged became extinct.

19 And the letter was a great volume, which was wholly written by the. finger of God:

20 And the name of the Father was on it, and of the Son and of the Holy Spirit, to rule for ever and ever. Hallelujah.

ODE 24

The mention of the Dove refers to a lost Gospel to which there are rare references in ancient writings.

1 The Dove fluttered over the Messiah, because He was her head; and she sang over Him and her voice was heard:

2 And the inhabitants were afraid and the sojourners were moved:

3 The birds dropped their wings and all creeping things died in their

holes: and the abysses were opened which had been hidden; and they cried to the Lord like women in travail:

4 And no food was given to them, because it did not belong to them;

5 And they sealed up the abysses with the seal of the Lord. And they perished, in the thought, those that had existed from ancient times;

6 For they were corrupt from the beginning; and the end of their corruption was life:

7 And every one of them that was imperfect perished: for it was not possible to give them a word that they might remain:

8 And the Lord destroyed the imaginations of all them that had not the truth with them.

9 For they who in their hearts were lifted up were deficient in wisdom, and so they were rejected, because the truth was not with them.

10 For the Lord disclosed His way, and spread abroad His grace: and those who understood it, know His holiness. Hallelujah.

ODE 25

Back again to personal experience.

1 I was rescued from my bonds and unto thee, my God, I fled:

2 For thou art the right hand of my Salvation and my helper.

3 Thou hast restrained those that rise up against me,

4 And I shall see him no more: because thy face was with me, which saved me by thy grace.

5 But I was despised and rejected in the eye of many: and I was in

their eyes like lead,

6 And strength was mine from thyself and help.

7 Thou didst set me a lamp at my right hand and at my left: and in me there shall be nothing that is not bright:

8 And I was clothed with the covering of thy Spirit, and thou didst remove from me my raiment of skin;

9 For thy right hand lifted me up and removed sickness from me:

10 And I became mighty in: the truth, and holy by thy righteousness; and all my adversaries were afraid of me;

11 And I became admirable by the name of the Lord, and was justified by His gentleness, and His rest is for ever and ever. Hallelujah.

ODE 26

Remarkable praise.

1 I poured out praise to the Lord, for I am His:

2 And I will speak His holy song, for my heart is with Him.

3 For His harp is in my hands, and the Odes of His rest shall not be silent.

4 I will cry unto him from my whole heart: I will praise and exalt Him with all my members.

5 For from the east and even to the west is His praise:

6 And from the south and even to the north is the confession of Him:

7 And from the top of the hills to their utmost bound is His perfection.

8 Who can write the Psalms of the Lord, or who read them?

9 Or who can train his soul for life, that his soul may be saved,

10 Or who can rest on the Most High, so that with His mouth he may speak?

11 Who is able to interpret the wonders of the Lord?

12 For he who could interpret would be dissolved and would become that which is interpreted.

13 For it suffices to know and to rest: for in rest the singers stand,

14 Like a river which has an abundant fountain, and flows to the help of them that seek it. Hallelujah.

ODE 27

The human body makes a cross when a man stands erect in prayer with arms outstretched.

1 I stretched out my hands and sanctified my Lord:

2 For the extension of my hands is His sign:

3 And my expansion is the upright tree [or cross].

ODE 28

This Ode is a musical gem.

1 As the wings of doves over their nestlings; and the mouth of their nestlings towards their mouths.

2 So also are the wings of the Spirit over my heart:

3 My heart is delighted and exults: like the babe who exults in the

womb of his mother:

4 I believed; therefore I was at rest; for faithful is He in whom I have believed:

5 He has richly blessed me and my head is with Him: and the sword shall not divide me from Him, nor the scimitar;

6 For I am ready before destruction comes; and I have been set on His immortal pinions:

7 And He showed me His sign: forth and given me to drink, and from that life is the spirit within me, and it cannot die, for it lives.

8 They who saw me marvelled at me, because I was persecuted, and they supposed that I was swallowed up: for I seemed to them as one of the lost;

9 And my oppression became my salvation; and I was their reprobation because there was no zeal in me;

10 Because I did good to every man I was hated,

11 And they came round me like mad dogs, who ignorantly attack their masters,

12 For their thought is corrupt and their understanding perverted.

13 But I was carrying water in my right hand, and their bitterness I endured by my sweetness;

14 And I did not perish, for I was not their brother nor was my birth like theirs.

15 And they sought for my death and did not find it: for I was older than the memorial of them;

16 And vainly did they make attack upon me and those who, without reward, came after me:

17 They sought to destroy the memorial of him who was before them.
18 For the thought of the Most High cannot be anticipated; and His heart is superior to all wisdom. Hallelujah.

ODE 29

Again reminiscent of the Psalms, of David.

1 The Lord is my hope: in Him I shall not be confounded.
2 For according to His praise He made me, and according to His goodness even so He gave unto me:
3 And according to His mercies He exalted me: and according to His excellent beauty He set me on high:
4 And brought me up out of the depths of Sheol: and from the mouth of death He drew me:
5 And thou didst lay my enemies low, and He justified me by His grace.
6 For I believed in the Lord's Messiah: and it appeared to me that He is the Lord;
7 And He showed him His sign: and He led me by His light, and gave me the rod of His power;
8 That I might subdue the imaginations of the peoples; and the power of the men of might to bring them low:
9 To make war by His word, and to take victory by His power.
10 And the Lord overthrew my enemy by His word: and he became like the stubble which the wind carries away;

11 And I gave praise to the Most High because He exalted me His servant and the son of His handmaid. Hallelujah.

ODE 30

An invitation to the thirsty.

1 Fill ye waters for yourselves from the living fountain of the Lord, for it is opened to you:
2 And come all ye thirsty, and take the draught; and rest by the fountain of the Lord.
3 For fair it is and pure and gives rest to the soul. Much more pleasant are its waters than honey;
4 And the honeycomb of bees is not to be compared with it.
5 For it flows forth from the lips of the Lord and from the heart of the Lord is its name.
6 And it came infinitely and invisibly: and until it was set in the midst they did not know it:
7 Blessed are they who have drunk therefrom and have found rest thereby. Hallelujah.

ODE 31

A song that Marcus Aurelius might have known when he said "Be like the promontory against which the waves continually break."

1 The abysses were dissolved before the Lord: and darkness was destroyed by His appearance:
2 Error went astray and perished at His hand: and folly found no path to walk in, and was submerged by the truth of the Lord.
3 He opened His mouth and spake grace and joy: and He spake a new song of praise to His name:
4 And He lifted up His voice to the Most High, and offered to Him the sons that were with Him.
5 And His face was justified, for thus His holy Father had given to Him.
6 Come forth, ye that have been afflicted and receive joy, and possess your souls by His grace; and take to you immortal life.
7 And they made me a debtor when I rose up, me who had been a debtor: and they divided my spoil, though nothing was due to them.
8 But I endured and held my peace and was silent, as if not, moved by them.
9 But I stood unshaken like a firm rock which is beaten by the waves and endures.
10 And I bore their bitterness for humility's sake:
11 In order, that I might redeem my people, and inherit it and that I

might not make void my promises to the fathers, to whom I promised the salvation of their seed. Hallelujah.

ODE 32

Joy and light.

1 To the blessed there is joy from their hearts, and light from Him that dwells in them:
2 And words from the Truth, who was self-originate: for He is strengthened by the holy power of the Most High: and He is unperturbed for ever and ever. Hallelujah.

ODE 33

A virgin stands and proclaims (v. 5).

1 Again Grace ran and forsook corruption, and came down in Him to bring it to nought;
2 And He destroyed perdition from before Him, and devastated all its order;
3 And He stood on a lofty summit and uttered His voice from one end of the earth to the other:
4 And drew to Him all those who obeyed Him; and there did not appear as it were an evil person.
5 But there stood a perfect virgin who was proclaiming and calling and saying,

6 O ye sons of men, return ye, and ye daughters of men, come ye:

7 And forsake the ways of that corruption and draw near unto me, and I will enter into you, and will bring you forth from perdition,

8 And make you wise in the ways of truth: that you be not destroyed nor perish:

9 Hear ye me and be redeemed. For the grace of God I am telling among you: and by my means you shall be redeemed and become blessed.

10 I am your judge; and they who have put me on shall not be injured: but they shall possess the new world that is incorrupt:

11 My chosen ones walk in me, and my ways I will make known to them that seek me, and I will make them trust in my name. Hallelujah.

ODE 34

True poetry--pure and simple.

1 No way is hard where there is a simple heart.

2 Nor is there any wound where the thoughts are upright:

3 Nor is there any storm in the depth of the illuminated thought:

4 Where one is surrounded on every side by beauty, there is nothing that is divided.

5 The likeness of what is below is that which is above; for everything is above: what is below is nothing but the imagination of those that are without knowledge.

6 Grace has been revealed for your salvation. Believe and live and be saved. Hallelujah.

ODE 35

"No cradled child more softly lies than I: come soon, eternity."

1 The dew of the Lord in quietness He distilled upon me:
2 And the cloud of peace He caused to rise over my head, which guarded me continually;
3 It was to me for salvation: everything was shaken and they were affrighted;
4 And there came forth from them a smoke and a judgment; and I was keeping quiet in the order of the Lord:
5 More than shelter was He to me, and more than foundation.
6 And I was carried like a child by his mother: and He gave me milk, the dew of the Lord:
7 And I grew great by His bounty, and rested in His perfection,
8 And I spread out my hands in the lifting up of my soul: and I was made right with the Most High, and I was redeemed with Him. Hallelujah.

ODE 36

Theologians have never agreed on an explanation of this perplexing Ode.

1 I rested in the Spirit of the Lord: and the Spirit raised me on high:
2 And made me stand on my feet in the height of the Lord, before His perfection and His glory, while I was praising Him by the composition of His songs.
3 The Spirit brought me forth before the face of the Lord: and, although a son of man, I was named the Illuminate, the Son of God:
4 While I praised amongst the praising ones, and great was I amongst the mighty ones.
5 For according to the greatness of the Most High, so He made me: and like His own newness He renewed me; and He anointed me from His own perfection:
6 And I became one of His Neighbours; and my mouth was opened, like a cloud of dew,
7 And my heart poured out as it were a gushing stream of righteousness,
8 And my access to Him was in peace; and I was established by the Spirit of His government. Hallelujah.

ODE 37

An elementary Ode.

1 I stretched out my hands to my Lord: and to the Most I High I raised my voice:

2 And I spake with the lips of my heart; and He heard me, when my voice reached I Him:

3 His answer came to me, and gave me the fruits of my labours;

4 And it gave me rest by the grace of the Lord. Hallelujah.

ODE 38

A beautiful description of the power of truth.

1 I went up to the light of truth as if into a chariot:

2 And the Truth took me and led me: and carried me across pits and gulleys; and from the rocks and the waves it preserved me:

3 And it became to me a haven of Salvation: and set me on the arms of immortal life:

4 And it went with me and made me rest, and suffered me not to wander, because it was the Truth;

5 And I ran no risk, because I walked with Him;

6 And I did not make an error in anything because I obeyed the Truth.

7 For Error flees away from it, and meets it not: but the Truth proceeds in the right path, and

8 Whatever I did not know, it made clear to me, all the poisons of

error, and the plagues of death which they think to be sweetness:

9 And I saw the destroyer of destruction, when the bride who is corrupted is adorned: and the bridegroom who corrupts and is corrupted;

10 And I asked the Truth 'Who are these?'; and He said to me, 'This is the deceiver and the error:

11 And they are alike in the beloved and in his bride: and they lead astray and corrupt the whole world:

12 And they invite many to the banquet,

13 And give them to drink of the wine of their intoxication, and remove their wisdom and knowledge, and so they make them without intelligence;

14 And then they leave them; and then these go about like madmen corrupting: seeing that-they are without heart, nor do they seek for it!

15 And I was made wise so as not to fall into the hands of the deceiver; and I congratulated myself because the Truth went with me,

16 And I was established and lived and was redeemed,

17 And my foundations were laid on the hand of the Lord: because He established me.

18 For He set the root and watered it and fixed it and blessed it; and its fruits are for ever.

19 It struck deep and sprung up and spread out, and was full and enlarged;

20 And the Lord alone was glorified in His planting and in His husbandry: by His care and by the blessing of His lips,

21 By the beautiful planting of His right hand: and by the discovery of His planting, and by the thought of His mind. Hallelujah.

ODE 39

One of the few allusions to events in the Gospels--that of our Lord walking on the Sea of Galilee.

1 Great rivers are the power of the Lord:
2 And they carry headlong those who despise Him: and entangle their paths:
3 And they sweep away their fords, and catch their bodies and destroy their lives.
4 For they are more swift than lightning and more rapid, and those who cross them in faith are not moved;
5 And those who walk on them without blemish shall not be afraid.
6 For the sign in them is the Lord; and the sign is the way of those who cross in the name of the Lord;
7 Put on, therefore, the name of the Most High, and know Him, and you shall cross without danger, for the rivers will be subject to you.
8 The Lord has bridged them by His word; and He walked and crossed them on foot:
9 And His footsteps stand firm on the water, and are not injured; they are as firm as a tree that is truly set up.
10 And the waves were lifted up on this side and on that, but the footsteps of our Lord Messiah stand firm and are not obliterated and are not defaced.

11 And a way has been appointed for those who cross after Him and for those who adhere to the course of faith in Him and worship His name. Hallelujah.

ODE 40

A song of praise without equal.

1 As the honey distills from the comb of the bees,

2 And the milk flows from the woman that loves her children;

3 So also is my hope on Thee, my God.

4 As the fountain gushes out its water,

5 So my heart gushes out the praise of the Lord and my lips utter praise to Him, and my tongue His psalms.

6 And my face exults with His gladness, and my spirit exults in His love, and my soul shines in Him:

7 And reverence confides in Him; and redemption in Him stands assured:

8 And His inheritance is immortal life, and those who participate in it are incorrupt. Hallelujah.

ODE 41

We discover that the writer may be a Gentile (v. 8).

1 All the Lord's children will praise Him, and will collect the truth of His faith.

2 And His children shall be known to Him. Therefore we will sing in His love:

3 We live in the Lord by His grace: and life we receive in His Messiah:

4 For a great day has shined upon us: and marvellous is He who has given us of His glory.

5 Let us, therefore, all of us unite together in the name of the Lord, and let us honour Him in His goodness,

6 And let our faces shine in His light: and let our hearts meditate in His love by night and by day.

7 Let us exult with the joy of the Lord.

8 All those will be astonished that see me. For from another race am I:

9 For the Father of truth remembered me: He who possessed me from the beginning:

10 For His bounty begat me, and the thought of His heart:

11 And His Word is with us in all our way;

12 The Saviour who makes alive and does not reject our souls-;

13 The man who was humbled, and exalted by His own righteousness,

14 The Son of the Most High appeared in the perfection of His Father;

15 And light dawned from the Word that was beforetime in Him;

16 The Messiah is truly one; and He was known before the foundation

of the world,

17 That He might save souls for ever by the truth of His name: a new song arises from those who love Him. Hallelujah.

ODE 42

The Odes of Solomon, the Son of David, are ended with the following exquisite verses.

1 I stretched out my hands and approached my Lord:
2 For the stretching of my hands is His sign:
3 My expansion is the outspread tree which was set up on the way of the Righteous One.
4 And I became of no account to those who did not take hold of me; and I shall be with those who love me.
5 All my persecutors are dead; and they sought after me who hoped in me, because I was alive:
6 And I rose up and am with them; and I will speak by their mouths.
7 For they have despised those who persecuted them;
8 And I lifted up over them the yoke of my love;
9 Like the arm of the bridegroom over the bride,
10 So was my yoke over those that know me:
11 And as the couch that is spread in the house of the bridegroom and bride,
12 So is my love over those that believe in me.
13 And I was not rejected though I was reckoned to be so.

14 I did not perish, though they devised it against me.
15 Sheol saw me and was made miserable:
16 Death cast me up, and many along with me.
17 I had gall and bitterness, and I went down with him to the utmost of his depth:
18 And the feet and the head he let go, for they were not able to endure my face:
19 And I made a congregation of living men amongst his dead men, and I spake with them by living lips:
20 Because my word shall not be void:
21 And those who had died ran towards me: and they cried and said, Son of God, have pity on us, and do with us according to thy kindness,
22 And bring us out from the bonds of darkness: and open to us the door by which we shall come out to thee.
23 For we see that our death has not touched thee.
24 Let us also be redeemed with thee: for thou art our Redeemer.
25 And I heard their voice; and my name I sealed upon their heads:
26 For they are free men and they are mine. Hallelujah.

www.ingramcontent.com/pod-product-compliance
Lightning Source LLC
Chambersburg PA
CBHW071654090426
42738CB00009B/1519